SO-ATQ-472

The Merrill Studies
in
Look Homeward, Angel

CHARLES E. MERRILL STUDIES

Under the General Editorship of
Matthew J. Bruccoli and Joseph Katz

The Merrill Studies
in
Look Homeward, Angel

Compiled by

Paschal Reeves
University of Georgia

Charles E. Merrill Publishing Company
A Bell & Howell Company
Columbus, Ohio

WITHDRAWN

Copyright © 1970 by Charles E. Merrill Publishing Company, Columbus, Ohio. All rights reserved. No part of this book may be reproduced
in any form, electronic or mechanical, including photocopy, recording,
or any information storage and retrieval system without permission in
writing from the publisher.

ISBN: 0-675-09354-6

Library of Congress Catalog Number: 70-119518

1 2 3 4 5 6 7 8 9 10 — 79 78 77 76 75 74 73 72 71 70

Printed in the United States of America

To

Edd Winfield Parks
1906-1968

702418

Preface

The year 1929 was a vintage year for the American novel. The culmination of the zaniest decade in the nation's history witnessed the appearance of William Faulkner's *The Sound and the Fury*, Ernest Hemingway's *A Farewell to Arms*, and Thomas Wolfe's *Look Homeward, Angel*. Although the winds of critical taste have blown both hot and cold on them, these three books remain as solid literary achievements and the passing of time has but enhanced their stature.

Unlike the other two, *Look Homeward, Angel* is a first novel; it is not however, the work of a novice. Before he began writing his first novel Wolfe spent six years in futile effort to become a successful playright, three of them as a member of George Pierce Baker's famed 47 Workshop at Harvard University. (It is one of the great ironies of the theatre that twenty years after his death *Look Homeward, Angel*, adapted into a play by the hand of another, had a long and successful run on Broadway.) After vain attempts to sell his plays *Mannerhouse* and *Welcome to Our City* in the spring of 1926, the frustrated playwright turned to fiction, and his prodigal talent found its *métier*. He began writing *Look Homeward, Angel* in England during the summer of 1926 and worked on it steadily until he completed the manuscript in New York in March 1928. The novel, at that time entitled *O Lost*, was promptly rejected by three publishers, and two others declined to consider it. Finally, in January 1929 Charles Scribner's Sons agreed to publish it. Wolfe then revised the manuscript and changed the title to *Look Homeward, Angel: A Story of the Buried Life*.

Look Homeward, Angel, priced at $2.50, was published on October 19, 1929; that was not a propitious time for an ambitious literary work to appear. Eleven days later on "Black Tuesday" the stock market crashed, and plunged the nation into the worst economic depression it has ever known. Despite this gathering storm of financial collapse, the book continued to make its way. Three weeks after publication a second printing was ordered, and the novel continued its slow but steady sales that have lasted for four decades. *Look Homeward, Angel* was never a best seller at home though it became one in both England and Germany. The Modern Library Edition was issued in 1934, the Grosset and Dunlap reprinted in 1939, and Scribner's has since brought out three other editions: an illustrated one in 1947, the Modern Standard Authors edition in 1952, and the Scribner Library Edition in 1960. Unlike other important novels that have dropped temporarily into oblivion to await future revival, *Look Homeward, Angel* has never been out of print and has never lacked for readers.

The response to *Look Homeward, Angel* ran the entire gamut from revulsion to admiration with all gradations in between. Wolfe's writing has always evoked strong emotional response in his readers and his first book was no exception. As a first novel by an unknown writer it was not widely reviewed by the newspapers, but it did receive attention from the more significant book-reviewing media. Some of the newspaper reviews were none too favorable and treated the book lightly. The first important review in a New York newspaper, Harry Hansen's in the *World,* was entitled "Ah, Life, Life!" and while he admitted the book gave "an impression of strength and promise" he went on to twit Wolfe for his "Meredethian prose" and "musing over destiny, fate, love ah me! ah me!" But the two most important newspapers, the *New York Times* and the *Herald-Tribune,* both gave the novel serious, thoughtful reviews that contributed greatly to its early success. Margaret Wallace in the *New York Times* recognized the originality, sensed the power, and prophetically concluded that "the final decision upon it, in all probability, rests with another generation than ours," and Margery Latimer in the *Herald-Tribune* found the book equally praiseworthy. These two reviews set *Look Homeward, Angel* on its way.

The magazine reviews, by and large, tended to reinforce the position taken by the two principal newspapers, except for an occasional strident dissent like Edwin Fairley's in the Unitarian *Christian Register.* Although the reviews had some reservations, they too praised Wolfe's achievement and expressed keen anticipation of his future work. John Chamberlain in *The Bookman* deplored some of Wolfe's rhetoric but declared that "No more sensuous novel has been written in the United States." Robert Reynolds in *Scribner's Magazine* compared Wolfe with Melville and Whitman, Geoffrey T. Helman marked his uniqueness in the *New Republic*, and Carl Van Doren praised his characterization in *Wings*. Representative of this combination of enthusiasm and qualification is the review by Basil Davenport in the *Saturday Review of Literature* that found in the book, despite its "faults of luxuriousness," a kinship with Rabelais in "a rare combination of fineness and largeness." Also illuminating is the review by Stringfellow Barr in the *Virginia Quarterly Review* that compares Wolfe's novel with one by an established Southern writer and issued by the same publisher, Stark Young's now-forgotten *River House*. Barr shrewdly cast his vote for the newcomer and hailed *Look Homeward, Angel* as a contribution to world literature.

When *Look Homeward, Angel* was published in London by Heinemann on July 14, 1930, it set off a British round of reviews that like their American counterparts spanned the entire range of response. Richard Aldington wrote a eulogistic review for the *Sunday Refree*, but Frank Swinnerton took the opposite position in the *Evening News*. Swinnerton declared "The book is a great jumble of good and bad . . . labored with adjectives and adverbs . . . emotional without feeling, crowded with violences and blasphemies, and to one reader appears incoherent, not from strength or intensity, but from over-excited verbosity." And Gerald Gould, as if trying to outdo Swinnerton, stated in the *Observer* that he could "see no reason why anybody should read" the novel. A more balanced review appeared in the influential *Times Literary Supplement*, and the opinion of its anonymous reviewer is more typical of the reaction of the English to *Look Homeward, Angel*. The disagreement about the novel, however, extended beyond the reviewers to the booksellers, some of whom refused to stock the book. The publisher quickly made capital of this action and advertised it in the *Times Literary Supplement*. Although *Look Homeward, Angel* never received the sales impetus of being banned in Boston, it did reap some notoriety in being banned by certain shops in London.

The reaction in London to *Look Homeward, Angel* was not even a tempest in a teapot compared to the furor it provoked in the author's hometown of Asheville, North Carolina. Wolfe's fiction is frankly autobiographical and his method of characterization was to draw his characteris from real life models. Though his characters underwent change and distortion through his creative imagination, the prototypes were not obscured in the process. The shock of recognition in Asheville when it discovered itself immortalized as Altamont resulted in outraged protest whose intensity startled the sensitive author. Nine years later, in a speech at Purdue University, Wolfe discussed Asheville's reception of his first novel: "Their outrage and anger, although mistaken, were unmistakable: there is no doubt that from the moment of the book's publication, I became an exile from my native town. I could not come back at that time, and it was seven years, in fact, before I wanted to come back, and did return." This reaction of Asheville to *Look Homeward, Angel* is vividly described by Floyd C. Watkins in "Save in His Own Country."

In sharp contrast to the storm at home was the stream of readers elsewhere who volunteered their praise of the book either by letter to Wolfe or in public utterance. Especially gratifying to him was the response of other writers. A visiting English novelist, Hugh Walpole, was quoted in a newspaper interview as saying: "His novel is as nearly perfect as a novel can be. I feel it a duty as a literary man to say something in his favor." And the chief American novelist provided the most dramatic endorsement the book received. Sinclair Lewis wrote Wolfe on October 23, 1930: "I wish there hadn't been quite so many brisk blurb-writers these past twenty years, using up every respectable phrase of literary criticism, so that I might have some fresh phrase with which to express my profound delight in *Look Homeward, Angel!* There is, you needn't be told, authentic greatness in it. It and *Farewell to Arms* seem to me to have more spacious power in them than any books for years, American OR foreign . . . . God, your book is good!" Two weeks later Lewis became the first American to win the Nobel Prize in Literature. At his press conference in New York after the announcement was made, Lewis expressed his admiration for *Look Homeward, Angel*, a sentiment he later repeated in his formal speech of acceptance before the Swedish Academy in Stockholm.

With publication in London *Look Homeward, Angel* had gone international, and Lewis's praise from his prestigious forum in Stockholm brought it to the attention of continental intellectuals, but it was not until translations were published in Europe that the novel became widely read there. During Wolfe's lifetime it appeared in four other European countries: Germany and Sweden in 1932, Norway in 1935, and Czechoslovakia in 1936. Since his death editions have been published in Denmark, Italy, Yugoslavia, France, and faraway Japan. Its reception in these countries has varied widely, from lukewarm in France to enthusiastic in Germany.

The history of *Look Homeward, Angel* in the United States provides another example of the buffeting that a literary masterpiece often receives before it gains its true recognition. Although the novel has never lacked in popular appeal, its critical course has been rocky indeed. Like other romantic works in the sociological thirties it received rough treatment from the Marxist-oriented critics. By the time their influence began to subside it became a target for another influential and largely hostile group, the formalist critics. Critical attacks by the Marxists and the formalists have been reinforced over the years by other detractors whose denegration was motivated neither by polemics nor aesthetics but rather by a personal animus against Wolfe himself or his later writing. While all this reaction has taken its toll of the novel's reputation there have been, on the other hand, able and perceptive critics who were not swayed by fashion nor misled by bias, and who recognized the enduring qualities of the novel. Writing in 1955, C. Hugh Holman surveys the first twenty-five years of the novel's history in "The Loneliness at the Core" and re-assesses its permanent worth.

Also damaging to the novel's reputation have been the widely circulated misconceptions about the role of the editor, Maxwell Perkins, in its publication. The length of the manuscript and its preparation for the press gave rise to numerous anecdotes that have long since passed into literary legend with all its distortion and exaggeration. Many of these legends, together with half-truths and outright fabrications, have masqueraded as fact and have become fixed in the public mind. Bernard DeVoto's vicious review in 1936 "Genius Is Not Enough," was widely interpreted as a retroactive attack on *Look Homeward, Angel* as well as a condemnation of *Of Time and the River*, and continued to fuel the rumor mills for years—long after it became common knowledge that the role of Perkins as editor was quite different in the two novels. Francis E. Skipp has subjected the editing of *Look Homeward, Angel* to a searching investigation, one that should lay the rumors permanently, but rumors like ghosts are difficult to exorcise. The results of his thorough research show that Perkins's editorial work on *Look Homeward, Angel* is similar to, and no greater than, that he did on the work of other Scribner authors he edited—be it Ernest Hemingway and Scott Fitzgerald, or Marjorie Kinnan Rawlings and Caroline Gordon. From the haze of myth and legend the fact has at last clearly emerged that *Look Homeward, Angel* was given its form and integrity by its author.

Yet another line of attack on *Look Homeward, Angel* has been to treat it as literal autobiography and to dismiss it as unworthy of serious consideration as fiction. Certainly no one can deny that the novel is autobiographical. The action covers the first twenty years of the author's life, its protagonist is an *alter ego*, the characters are drawn from his family and community, and the setting is his hometown. Such is the substance of autobiography, and in the hands of a lesser writer it might well have become just another superficial account of a boy who grows up in a small town and leaves to seek his fortune in the metropolis. But personal experience is also the material of fiction, and when filtered through a creative imagination and shaped by an artist, it ceases to be mere autobiography but becomes considerably more and takes on new dimensions, as James Joyce, D. H. Lawrence, Marcel Proust, and many others have shown. While a reader's response to the various types of fiction may be determined largely by taste, it is a critical fallacy of the first magnitude to fail to distinguish between pure autobiography and autobiographical fiction. In Wolfe's case, however, the position of critics who consider his work just autobiography has been enhanced, ironically, by his admirers, who, fascinated by the autobiographical quality of his writing, have themselves written much on prototypes, parallels, analogues, and comparisons between his fiction and real life—even though they recognize the fictional value of his work. Although the dust of all the critical skirmishes has not yet settled, it is apparent that *Look Homeward, Angel* is a novel and as such it must be judged as fiction. Autobiographical fiction it assuredly is, but still fiction, and it is no more accurate to consider it literal autobiography than it is to maintain that *Moby Dick* is but the account of Melville's life on a whaler or that *A Farewell to Arms* is only the military record of Ernest Hemingway in World War I. "Fiction," Caroline Gordon and Allen Tate once wrote, "differs from all other arts in that it concerns the conduct of life itself." And it is *life* itself rather than *a* life that is the concern of the fictional dimensions of *Look Homeward, Angel*.

These dimensions prove to be extensive indeed when they are explored judiciously. Although Wolfe has put unwary critics to the severest test of any writer since Whitman, as C. Hugh Holman maintains, he has also provided a challenge to serious critics that has not gone unanswered. In time there has evolved a body of informed and judicious criticism of *Look Homeward, Angel* that illuminates the novel as fiction. Representative, but by no means inclusive, of this enlightened and enlightening criticism are the selections given in this collection. The limitations of space have caused the omission of other worthy studies that the editor would have liked to include. A comprehensive bibliography of this significant criticism may be found in *The Merrill Checklist of Thomas Wolfe.*

Two significant appraisals of *Look Homeward, Angel* examine the fictional dimensions of the novel from different points of view. The earlier of these appeared in *Writers in Crisis* (1942), part of Maxwell Geismar's multi-volume history of the American novel, where he devotes more than fifty pages to Wolfe's work. Here Geismar views *Look Homeward, Angel* in the broad context of the novel in America and finds it to be a diary of the artist in America, especially provincial America, that is powerful and unique. While the study places some rather surprising strictures on Wolfe as a Southerner, it nevertheless is an affirmative evaluation of the novel and, coming when it did, has proved to be an influential starting point in the understanding of *Look Homeward, Angel.* Richard Walser's "Look Homeward, Angel" comes from his book in the American Authors and Critics Series that is intended as an introductory interpretation. However, Walser brings to his task a sympathetic understanding of *Look Homeward, Angel* based on great familiarity with the entire work and milieu of Wolfe and a prolonged study of the novel itself. Though he declares the central theme to be the familiar revolt from the village, and by inference an attack on provincialism, he subtly pursues the deeper meaning of the sensitive individual caught in life's prison-house, the resulting alienation, and the relevance of its lyrical expression in the novel.

After the publication of *Look Homeward, Angel,* Wolfe donned the mantle of the American bard, and his work throbbed to the epic impulse as he sought to capture the essence of the American character and the American experience in fiction. While this heroic intent is not altogether lacking in *Look Homeward, Angel,* Wolfe's main concern in his first novel is the individual self—the odyssey of self-discovery and the ordeal of acquiring self-knowledge. It is this fact that invests the story of Eugene Gant with its universality and its timelessness; the odyssey and the ordeal of the self know neither clime nor epoch but are the common experience of man. Into this search for understanding and meaning in life, Wolfe interwove a number of themes, at times readily drawn in bold relief but at others momentarily obscured by artistic design, often his lyrical and richly rhetorical expression. Even as a single thread can be followed in variegated cloth by a persistent eye, so can the perceptive critic isolate and define a single theme. In common with all great literary works, *Look Homeward, Angel* cannot be exhausted in one reading and further study reveals greater thematic diversity. And these varied themes are enriched by an evocative style and abundant symbolism. In the general studies in Part II and the specialized essays of Part III all of the main themes of the novel are discussed and many of the subordinate ones are touched upon. While there is no single article that is fully adequate on either the style or the symbolism of *Look Homeward, Angel,* a number of the writers deal with these matters in the context of their special concerns, so that the collection as a whole provides adequate discussion of these important aspects of the novel.

Although there is no agreement on a single theme as major, to the exclusion of all others, one of the terms most frequently applied to *Look Homeward, Angel* is *Bildungsroman* because the idea of growth is central to any valid interpretation of the novel. In "Wolfe's *Look Homeward, Angel* as a novel of Development," Richard S. Kennedy examines this fundamental concept and the means Wolfe employed to make it a classic example of this ancient type. But this eminently readable book is much more than an agonizing search for maturity; and part of its charm—as B. R. McElderry, Jr. points out in "The Durable Humor of *Look Homeward, Angel*"-comes from the rich vein of humor, a characteristic of the novel that has been unduly neglected. Though the humor has not received the attention it merits, less happy motifs have been more frequently treated. In "The Titles of *Look Homeward, Angel: A Story of the Buried Life.*" W. P. Albrecht considers isolation, the great theme of twentieth-century literature, as Wolfe develops it. Larry Rubin deals with the haunting and elusive concept of pre-existence in "Thomas Wolfe and the Lost Paradise." And the somber shadow cast in the novel by death, and its ramifications, are examined by J. Russell Reaver and Robert I. Strozier in "Thomas Wolfe and Death." The next two essays are concerned with more controversial aspects of the novel. Though many literary influences on Wolfe have been cited, in "The Grotesques of

Anderson and Wolfe," Louis J. Budd not only points out an important one that was long overlooked, but in treating *Look Homeward, Angel* as a book of the grotesque he places it in a long tradition of Southern writing from Edgar Allen Poe to Flannery O'Connor. And in "Eugene Gant and the Ghost of Ben" John S. Hill seeks to explain the final chapter of the novel, about which any general critical agreement is lacking.

Finally, there are three additional facets of the novel that demand attention. In "Thomas Wolfe: Time and the South," Louis D. Rubin, Jr. deals with two of them. Wolfe's compelling concern with time has not only attracted much critical attention but was in fact commented on by Wolfe himself in *The Story of a Novel*, and the vast importance of his Southern heritage is irrefutable. In this essay, a chapter of his book on writers of the modern South, Rubin also clearly delineates the process of alienation in the novel. The remaining idea, the quest for the unattainable, is presented in Pamela Hansford Johnson's "The Incommuncable Prison," the final chapter of her booklength study of Wolfe's art. Writing from the vantage point of a perceptive and knowledgeable European, as well as that of a fine creative artist herself, she assesses Wolfe's artistic achievement and the permanent value of his contribution to American literature.

On the eve of the publication of *Look Homeward, Angel* the anxious young author asked his editor what the verdict on the novel would be. Maxwell Perkins's reply proved to be as prophetic of the future as it was reassuring at that time: "The book will find its way." Indeed it has.

Paschal Reeves

Contents

2. Critical Appraisal: The Novel as a Whole

3. Critical Analysis: The Major Themes

The Merrill Studies
in
Look Homeward, Angel

Thomas Wolfe

Prologue: The Author's Intent

1. The earliest record of Thomas Wolfe's decision to write an autobiographical novel:

> The Book shall have this unity—it shall represent the struggle of a man to stand alone and apart—such a man as would be forced to stand alone by his physical and spiritual structure.

2. In progress:

> I am weary of the old forms—the old language—It has come to me quite simply these last three days that we must mine deeper— find language again in its primitive sinews—like the young man, Conrad—Joyce gets it at times in *Ulysses*—it is quite simple, but terrific. Build the book brick by brick.

From *The Notebooks of Thomas Wolfe,* edited by Richard S. Kennedy and Paschal Reeves. Copyright © 1970 by The University of North Carolina Press. Reprinted by permission of The University of North Carolina Press, and Richard S. Kennedy and Paschal Reeves.

1. Contemporary Response

Harry Hansen

Ah, Life! Life!

Among the first novels that give me an impression of strength and promise is "Look Homeward, Angel," by Thomas Wolfe, an instructor in New York University. It is a big, fat novel in the Thackeray manner about a commonplace American family in a drab American town. There is rich emotion in it, there is understanding sympathy in it, and there is in it the presence of an author who is aware of himself and his theme, who is more than a recorder.

Many new novels reject everything that this author includes. The young men and women who are making a record of life as it is, whether of actions or mental attitudes (Gertrude Diamant, John Riordan, Josephine Herbst, for example), are not interested in taking the roofs off houses and looking in, or in taking the tops off skulls and watching the convolutions of the brain. They report, for the most part, objectively; they eliminate non-essentials; they take for granted that ages of novel-writing have put the reader in the possession of aspects, points of view, attitudes that we take for granted. Not so Thomas Wolfe.

From the New York *World,* October 26, 1929, p. 15. Reprinted by permission of Harry Hansen.

4

When I opened "Look Homeward, Angel," and read the author's apology for using real people out of the old home town — transmuted, of course, for his novel — I knew that he would have his say. He used a whole page to announce what most authors put into a sentence: "Many of these characters are reminders of actual people, but although all are reminiscent, none is an actual portrait." Even that has been simplified by many authors to a line that protects them from libel suits: "The characters in this book are entirely imaginary."

But Mr. Wolfe is determined to do a full portrait. He has behind him, as internal evidence shows, the range of English literature. He knows Thackeray's manner (in his worst writing) of jumping into the text. He knows George Meredith's musings over destiny, fate, love, ah me! ah me! He is able to sprinkle phrases out of English authors into his pages without quotation marks, without references to footnotes, and thereby paying his reader the compliment of intelligence. He observes behavior, but to him behavior is not enough.

So "Look Homeward, Angel," becomes a rather formidable book, loaded down with details about the family of the Gants — about Gant, the father, who made tombstones in the provincial town of Altamont; and Eliza, the mother, who, after a protracted period of childbearing, opened a boarding house; and Eugene, the son. All egotists in their own way, all going forward to what? "Look Homeward, Angel," is a negation of any plan in life. This family sprawls, uses up its best talents without direction, finds its vitality spent in frustrated efforts, gets nowhere. On the wife's side were the Pentlands — "that strange, rich clan, with its fantastic mixture of success and impracticality, its hard moneyed sense, its visionary fanaticism." To this end the elder Gant, who had drowned in liquor his protest at the imprisonment of the spirit, did not belong. His son Eugene felt its irony and futility in greater measure, as neither of his two adolescent ambitions — to be loved and to be famous — proved the origin of lasting happiness.

All those varied forces that make for the success and the failure of American life are here brought to bear on the fortunes of a single family, and on one man, Eugene, the lad whose romantic appraisal of life was gradually worn down by defeat. We follow him in his Odyssey, half of the mind, half of the body, and watch him beating on the great door that imprisons life. What message has life to give him? The best of his discovery comes with the words of his dead brother, who appears to him to say that there is no happy land, no end to hunger. "You are your world," says Ben. The only lesson Eliza gains from life comes also at the end when she parts with Eugene: "We must try to love one another." In his Meredithian prose Wolfe continues: "The terrible and beautiful sentence, the last, the final wisdom that the earth can give, is remembered at the end, is spoken too late, wearily. It stands there, awful and traduced, above the dusty racket of our lives. No forgetting, no forgiving, no denying, no explaining, no hating. O mortal and perishing love, born with this flesh and dying with this brain, your memory will haunt the earth forever."

Moralizing such as this has been absent from novels these thirty years. In the days of James Lane Allen it became a bit cloying. To-day it is something of a surprise. Mr. Wolfe's commendable strength makes criticism seem captious. He has glaring defects, chief of which seems to be a lack of clearness at the beginning. He treats Oliver Gant so sympathetically that we have difficulty believing his excesses when they occur. But apparently his aim is to portray life without directing the feelings of the reader against any one character. Toward the whole he has the forgiveness that comes with understanding. His second novel will tell us whether he has staying power as a novelist, whether he will be more than a one-book man.

Margaret Wallace

A Novel of Provincial
American Life

Here is a novel of the sort one is too seldom privileged to welcome. It is a book of great drive and vigor, of profound originality, of rich and variant color. Its material is the material of every-day life, its scene is a small provincial Southern city, its characters are the ordinary persons who come and go in our daily lives. Yet the color of the book is not borrowed; it is native and essential. Mr. Wolfe has a very great gift—the ability to find in simple events and in humble, unpromising lives the whole meaning and poetry of human existence. He reveals to us facets of observation and depths of reality hitherto unsuspected, but he does so without outraging our notions of truth and order. His revelations do not startle. We come upon them, instead, with an almost electric sense of recognition.

The plot, if the book can be said to have a plot at all, is at once too simple and too elaborate to relate in synopsis. "Look Homeward, Angel" is a chronicle of a large family, the Gants of Altamont, over a period of twenty years. In particular, it is the chronicle of Eugene

From the *New York Times Book Review*, October 27, 1929, p. 7. Copyright © 1929, 1957 by the New York Times Company. Reprinted by permission of *The New York Times*.

Gant, the youngest son, who entered the world in 1900. W. O. Gant was a stonecutter, a strong, turbulent, sentimental fellow, given to explosions of violent and lavish drunkenness, and to alternating fits of whining hypochondria. Eliza Gant, his second wife and the mother of his family, was an executive woman with a passion for pinching pennies and investing shrewdly in real estate. The Gants grew in age and prosperity with the growth of the sprawling mountain town of Altamont.

By 1900 the Gants were firmly and prosperously established in Altamont—although under the shadow of the father's whining dread of the tax collector, they continued to live as if poverty and destitution lay just around the corner. They kept a cheap, garish boarding house called Dixieland, living their daily lives on the fringe of a world of paying guests whose necessities had to be considered first. Eugene Gant grew from childhood into an awkward and rather withdrawn adolescence, hedged about by the turbulent lives of his family and singularly lonely in the midst of them. Indeed, each of the Gants was lonely in a separate fashion. Mr. Wolfe, in searching among them for the key to their hidden lives, comes upon no unifying fact save that of isolation.

Through the book like the theme of a symphony runs the note of loneliness and of a groping, defeated search for an answer to the riddle of eternal solitude.

> Naked and alone we come into exile. In her dark womb we did not know our mother's face; from the prison of her flesh have we come into the unspeakable and incommunicable prison of this earth. Which of us has known his brother? Which of us has looked into his father's heart? Which of us has not remained forever prison-pent? Which of us is not forever a stranger and alone?

Eugene grew into life hating its loneliness and desolation, its lack of meaning, its weariness and stupidity, the ugliness and cruelty of its lusts. For the rawness and evil of life was early apparent to him —hanging about the depressing miscellaneous denizens of Dixieland, delivering his papers in Niggertown, growing up in the streets and alleys of Altamont. He found a poignant beauty in it, too— the simple beauty of things seen in youth, the more elusive beauty to be found in books, and later, after his years at college and the death of his brother Ben, the terrible beauty flowering from pain and ugliness. But always there remained in him that loneliness, and an obscure and passionate hunger which seemed to him a part of the giant rhythm of the earth.

"Look Homeward, Angel" is as interesting and powerful a book as has ever been made out of the drab circumstances of provincial American life. It is at once enormously sensuous, full of the joy and gusto of life, and shrinkingly sensitive, torn with revulsion and disgust. Mr. Wolfe's style is sprawling, fecund, subtly rhythmic and amazingly vital. He twists language masterfully to his own uses, heeding neither the decency of a word nor its licensed existence, so long as he secures his sought for and instantaneous effect. Assuredly, this is a book to be savored slowly and reread, and the final decision upon it, in all probability, rests with another generation than ours.

Margery Latimer

The American Family

Sometimes an intense shock or a pain that has to be endured will give you a monstrous delight in life, as if the cautious habitual self in you had had its death blow and you were thrown out of yourself into the universe. This book is like that. There is such mammoth appreciation of experience and of living that the intention of the novel cannot be articulated. It comes through to you like fumes or like one supreme mood of courage that you can never forget, and with it all the awe, the defilement and grandeur of actual life. Mr. Wolfe makes you experience a family through twenty years of its existence. He gives the disharmony, the joy, the hideous wastefulness and the needless suffering, and yet not once do you dare shrink from life and not once are you plastered with resentment and loathing for reality and experience. The author has stated in his introduction that he wrote this book with strong joy, not counting the costs, and I believe it. He also has said he tried to comprehend his people not by telling what they did but what they should have done.

From the New York *Herald Tribune Books,* November 3, 1929, p. 20. Reprinted by permission of W. C. C. Publishing Company, Inc., copyright owner.

10

This "should-have-done" is the lyrical, subtle part of the book that comes to you in moments of peril. Ben, the elder brother, finally dies. He has never been educated because of his mother's iron determination to own all the real estate in Altamont and his father's riotous capacity for enjoyment. His whole being has been at the mercy of his parent's whims and the working out of their characters. As he dies the terrible vanity of the family rises above the calamity, their desire to vindicate themselves shuts him out of the world and finally, as they reveal themselves, you reach the rock bottom of their characters—innocence. Compared to some rational, ideal pattern of living they are mad, insane, as innocent as animals who kill each other for food and cannot do otherwise.

"Then, over the ugly clamor of their dissension, over the rasp and snarl of their nerves, they heard the low mutter of Ben's expiring breath. The light had been reshaded; he lay like his own shadow, in all his fierce gray lonely beauty. And as they looked and saw his bright eyes already blurred with death, and saw the feeble beating flutter of his poor thin breast, the strange wonder, the dark rich miracle of his life surged over them its enormous loveliness. They grew quiet and calm, they plunged below all the splintered wreckage of their lives, they drew together in a superb communion of love and valiance, beyond horror and confusion, beyond death!"

Eugene, the youngest son, suddenly understands and possesses his family for a moment. As he looks at his brother he thinks, "That was not all! That really was not all!" And you think, reading, "O lost! that part of people that cannot be understood or possessed or expressed, O lost world of people—each one mysterious." But every act of these people is inevitable, so are their clothes, so are their words. Stevie, for example, "J. T. Collins, that's who! He's only worth about two hundred thousand. 'Steve,' he said, just like that, 'if I had your brains'—he would continue in this way with moody self-satisfaction, painting a picture of future success when all who scorned him now would flock to his standard." And Eliza at the very beginning does not need to be described when she says, "If I'd been there, you can bet your bottom dollar there'd been no loss. Or, it'd be on the other side." And then Gant, who part of the time is "picked foul and witless from the cobbles" and the rest of the time is making his house roar with fires and rich talk, making the outside of his house rich with vines and carving angels on grave stones. Or he is bringing into the warm kitchen great bundles of meat.

In them all, like the vast crude breathing of the earth, is their will to live. Mr. Wolfe describes with monstrous torrential joy the

sensual delights of eating. He isn't content to describe a meal in a
sentence, but he uses a page, bringing the food before you until it
is so tangible it is intolerable, until it is so rich and abundant that
it pierces you with awe of life. All the time you are eating that food
as if it were actual. He describes the monstrous pleasures of the
body in the same way until there is a gigantic picture of living flesh
enjoying the universe. But like a Greek chorus or an angelic whisper
from the center of this excess are the words, "O lost!"

The story is always present. There is always the tremendous
excitement of the life of this family, of what they will do and say
and feel. Eugene, who in the author's mind is the central character
of the book, is interesting only in connection with his family. The
story is really the family with its distorted relationships shadowed
by their angelic possibilities. Each person is a distinct reality but
they are bound together, and when they are sundered the life of
the book dwindles. Eugene at college is not as interesting or as real
as Eugene the paper boy trying to collect from the prostitutes in
Niggertown. But Eugene's life away from his family is only one
hundred pages or so, and the fact that Ben's death marks the highest point in feeling and interest does not diminish the value of the
book as a whole. The author proudly and naively says "It sometimes
seems to me that this book presents a picture of American life that
I have never seen elsewhere." I agree with him, and if I could create
now one magic word that would make everyone want to read the
book I would write it down and be utterly satisfied.

Basil Davenport

C'est Maître François

If it were customary to head reviews with a motto, like a chapter of Walter Scott, a review of "Look Homeward, Angel" might well take a phrase from Mr. Arthur Machen's "The Street Glory": *"C'est Maître François! Maître François en très mauvais humeur peut-être, mais Maître François tout de même!"* The analogy must not be pushed too far; there are of course many important differences, notably a violent emotional intensity in Mr. Wolfe that is entirely lacking in Rabelais, but they have the same fundamental and most unusual quality, a robust sensitiveness. Extraordinary keenness of perception usually makes a character like Roderick Usher or Des Esseintes, or, in real life, Proust, one who is forced to shut himself away from bright lights, loud sounds, and strong feelings, and occupies himself with infinitely cautious and delicate experiments upon himself. But Mr. Wolfe, like Rabelais, though plainly odors and colors and all stimuli affect him more intensely than most people, is happily able to devour sensations with an enormous vigor; his perceptions have a rare combination of fineness and largeness.

From the *Saturday Review of Literature,* VI (December 21, 1929), 584. Reprinted by permission of the *Saturday Review.*

In manner, Mr. Wolfe is most akin to James Joyce, somewhere
between the ascetic beauty of the "Portrait of the Artist as a Young
Man" and the unpruned fecundity of "Ulysses"; but he resembles
many other people by turns. His hero, Eugene Gant, amuses himself
by registering at country hotels as John Milton or William Blake,
or by asking for a cup of cold water and blessing the giver in his
Father's name; so Mr. Wolfe amuses himself by writing here in the
manner of one author and there of another. He will suddenly fall
into a dada fantasia, such as often appears in *transition*, as:

> A woman sobbed and collapsed in a faint. She was immediately
> carried out by two Boy Scouts . . . who administered first aid to her
> in the rest-room, one of them hastily kindling a crackling fire of pine
> boughs by striking two flints together, while the other made a tour-
> niquet, and tied several knots in his handkerchief,—

and so on, and half a dozen pages later he will enumerate, in the
painfully unimaginative manner of "An American Tragedy," the
real holdings of Mrs. Gant:

"There were, besides, three good building-lots on Merrion Avenue
valued at $2,000 apiece, or at $5,500 for all three; the house on
Woodson Street valued at $5,000," and so on for a page and a half.
That is, it seems to be the great gift of Mr. Wolfe that everything
is interesting, valuable, and significant to him. It must be confessed
that he has just missed the greatest of gifts, that of being able to
convey his interest to the ordinary reader.

Upon what was his vitality nourished? Rabelais fed on all the
fulness of the French Renaissance, a dawn in which it was bliss to
be alive; what would he have been like if he had been a poor boy in
a small southern town, with a drunken father, a shrewish mother,
and a family of quarreling brothers and sisters? Mr. Wolfe's answer
seems to be that, in his childhood at least, he would have done
unexpectedly well. Eugene, in pitifully cramped surroundings, somehow has a greater fulness of life than most boys have. From his
father, especially, he draws some sense of Dionysian madness, of
Falstaffian greatness. The teaching he has is very bad, but he gets
somewhere, from it or from himself, a real feeling for Latin and
Greek. His first money is earned on a paper route that takes him
through the negro quarter, his first knowledge of women comes from
a negress who is in arrears to his company, yet he is never without
a sense of the wonder and pain of desire and hunger. Years ago Mr.
Tarkington said: "There's just as many kinds of people in Kokomo
as there is in Pekin," but he carried little conviction, for his melo-

drama was too obviously arranged. It is Mr. Wolfe's contribution that he has drawn an unsparing picture of character and emotion. For those who can see it, there is everywhere a wealth of vitality that is almost enough.

But it is the little less, after all, and his town grows more insufficient as Eugene grows older. There is one chapter, in manner probably inspired by "The Waste Land," describing an afternoon in the square, with a running comment of quotations.

> "Give me a dope, too."
> "I don't want anything," said Pudge Carr. Such drinks as made them nobly wild, not mad. . .
> Mrs. Thelma Jarvis, the milliner, drew, in one swizzling guzzle, the last beaded chain of linked sweetness long drawn out from the bottom of her glass. Drink to me only with thine eyes. . . . She writhed carefully among the crowded tables, with a low rich murmur of contrition. Her voice was ever soft, gentle, and low—an excellent thing in a woman. The high light chatter of the tables dropped as she went by. For God's sake, hold your tongue and let me love!

It is good enough, the town and the soda-water, but it should be so much better! A great company of poets are called on to set the beauties of the world against their pitiful analogues in Altamont. Mr. Wolfe's criticism of the narrowness of his hero's surroundings is the more bitter because he has done it such abundant justice.

The bitterness grows when Eugene goes to the state university. Here Eugene, developing rapidly, becomes more difficult to understand, more difficult perhaps for his author to picture. It is often observable in books that begin with the birth of a boy that they grow confused as he approaches the age of the author. Here too the goat-foot that always belongs to the followers of Joyce is shown. Eugene becomes morbidly conscious of his physique, and yet unnaturally neglectful of it. He does not have his teeth filled or his hair cut; he does not bathe. He is naturally not popular, and he resents his want of popularity, in a way that is not far short of megalomania; he revolts against American sanitation and cleanliness, declaring that health is for fools, and great men have always shown signs in their lined faces of the disease of genius. Now this is hardly comprehensible, and hence hardly credible, even when the first two thirds of the book has given one the will to be as sympathetic as possible. There are possible reasons for Eugene's cult of dirt, ranging from a subconscious fear of impotence and a confused desire to be like the Horatian he-goat, *elentis mariti* (there is something like that in

Mr. D. H. Lawrence), to a rankling sense of social inferiority, perverted by a fierce pride into a resolve to emulate the Fraternity Row aristocracy in nothing, not even in cleanliness (there is something like that in Mr. Wilbur Daniel Steele's "Meat"), through a dozen others. But Eugene here is not clear, as if Mr. Wolfe did not understand him, or understood him too well to think him worth explaining.

In the end Eugene is left wondering, with the same sense of the loneliness and greatness of the soul that informs the book from the beginning. "Look Homeward, Angel" though it has the faults of luxuriousness, has the great virtue that it always has the vision of something half-comprehensible behind the humdrum life, and that in the reading it carries conviction with it.

E[dwin] F[airley]

Look Homeward, Angel

We gather from the jacket that the publishers kept this book three years before they published it. In our judgment, they ought to have burned it. It is the small-town life of a small-town family of futilitarians. But why write of them? They could swear, and visit brothels, and quarrel no end; but what of it? Even the similes in this foul book are vile. Why? To mirror life? We could stand a little low life if there was some high ideals; but this book has none. We confess a supreme distaste for such sentences as "Came a day," and the man's vocabulary is beyond us. Here are some words culled at random: "alexin," "octopal," "funky," "convolved," "conspirate," "gabular," "adyts," "bigged," "calvered"; but why go on? One disgusting situation follows another until we are nauseated. Why did a reputable house put out such a book?

From *The Christian Register,* CIX (January 9, 1930), 31. Reprinted by permission of *UUA NOW,* successor to *The Christian Register.*

Stringfellow Barr

The Dandridges
and the Gants

Stark Young's "River House" and Thomas Wolfe's "Look Home-ward, Angel" are both novels about the South written by South-erners. But a foreigner would not readily discover in the two books reflections of the same civilization. "River House" is a backward glance at a dying culture submerged and overwhelmed not merely by America but by its own Americanized youth. "Look Homeward, Angel" is the saga of a human soul, the soul of a boy who happened to grow up in North Carolina.

Many of Mr. Young's most ardent admirers have doubted whether the novel was his true métier: it has been in his dramatic criticism, his "encaustics," his vignettes that they felt most the force of his personality, a personality rich in artistic sincerity, in restraint, in spiritual discretions. But I think that in "River House" Mr. Young has done a valuable piece of work and one that could have been done in no other form. Who else in America is so well fitted to portray the conflict between the older South and its Americanized offspring? And how surely he has placed his finger on the real tragedy of that conflict: not that — as Major Dandridge

From the *Virginia Quarterly Review,* VI (Spring 1930), 310-313. Reprinted by permission of the *Virginia Quarterly Review* and Stringfellow Barr.

of River House would have put it — the South was defeated but not beaten, but that Major Dandridge's daughter-in-law did not know how many years it took to get from Fort Sumter to Appomattox. Mr. Young paints with infinite lovingness the aging inmates of River House: the Major, Aunt Ellen, Aunt Rosa, the horsey Mr. Bobo, the vatic "Cud'n Tom." The old ladies, particularly, are genuine miniature masterpieces. But Mr. Young knows also the incoherent agony of young John Dandridge's heart; he knows why the young Southerner finds Southern family life with its garrulous intrusions so extremely oppressive; he knows why John's wife, who seems to the Major no better than she ought to be, finds the older sexual ethic of the South really obscene. "River House" is not an important novel, but it is filled with understanding.

I should call "Look Homeward, Angel" the work of a genius, but that the word is somewhat overworn of late. In any case I believe it is the South's first contribution to world literature. I am aware that "Uncle Remus" is read wherever English is spoken and that in our own generation writers like DuBose Heyward and Julia Peterkin have created real literature. But it seems to me extremely significant that generally speaking the Southern writer has had to turn to the negro when he wanted to paint life as it is. The life of the white Southerner has been for political and traditional reasons so compact of legal fictions and dying social shibboleths that it has been difficult to do anything with it unless one sentimentalized. Even "River House" had to be composed in a minor key, perhaps the only key available to a defeated culture. Thomas Wolfe, on the other hand, has constructed a really tremendous novel out of the mean and sordid life of a North Carolina town. A lesser artist looking on that scene, would have become excitedly denunciatory or triumphantly analytical and would have discovered in it no more than another Zenith City or another Winesburg, Ohio. What Mr. Wolfe beheld was the travail of the human spirit, blind to its own stupidities, its cowardice, its lusts. His novel is of epic proportions, physically and spiritually.

His hero's father "reeled down across the continent" from Pennsylvania to North Carolina and spawned a family of children as terrifyingly different from each other as most brothers and sisters really are: Helen, with her tempestuous affections and antagonisms and her inherited bibulous tendencies; Luke, with his genius for acquaintance and his incapacity for real feeling; Steve, whining, boasting, and stinking of nicotine; Eugene, about whom this epic really centers; Ben, with this fierce spiritual isolation, perpetually murmuring over his shoulder to his particular angel: "God! Listen to that, won't you!" Above them all the father, W. O. Gant, towers like the elder Karamazov, screaming profanity and obscenity at his wife and children, reciting eternally from Shakespeare and a dozen other bards, roaring for every one's pity, drinking himself into cancer, and being hauled out of brothels by his eldest son.

Which of Thomas Wolfe's particular skills has contributed most to this book's making? Over and over again his prose slips into sheer poetry. Over and over again one ironic sentence creates a character. But above all his loving pity for all of lost humanity gives his work that religious quality one gets in Dostoevsky.

Does Mr. Wolfe add anything to our comprehension of the South? It is a difficult question to answer. His book is not about the South of Major Dandridge at all. Indeed, that Old South is not very obvious to anybody who ever saw "Altamont," which is the name Mr. Wolfe gives his native Asheville. The Gants are certainly not typical of the Southern upper class, though neither are they quite what that upper class means by "common." They are socially unclassifiable. "Look Homeward, Angel" is not concerned with the problem of a surviving Southern culture. When its author mentions the South it is chiefly to speak of "the exquisite summer of the South," the "opulent South," or the "fabulous South." The natural beauty of the land lies deep in his blood but the politico-social problems of its people touch him scarcely at all.

I do not believe that Mr. Wolfe's novel has invalidated one iota the significance of whatever the Old South produced of human beauty; and I am certain that Mr. Wolfe himself would feel soiled at being thought of as a "debunker." But I do think that he is the first novelist of the new dispensation in the Southern States, the first to grow up sufficiently outside of River House to look with a child's eyes at the life about him. Whenever, as in Poland or Italy or Ireland, the sense of a culture distorted by outside pressure has directed the artist's eyes to programs like national resurgence, the highest art has been the chief sufferer. The South has labored precisely under that handicap; unable to recapture a social synthesis that Reconstruction had destroyed, it had not the heart, or the stomach either, to adopt frankly the American solution of life. Nor has Mr. Wolfe adopted it, but his conflict is no longer the political conflict of the South and the North but the artistic conflict of his own spirit with the souls about him. With "Look Homeward, Angel" the South has contributed to the literature of the world a novel, strongly provincial in its flavor, universal in its terrible tragedy.

Look Homeward, Angel

Mr. Thomas Wolfe's novel, LOOK HOMEWARD, ANGEL (Heinemann, 10s. 6d. net), was obviously written as the result of tremendous internal pressure. It is a first novel and very long, following a boy's emergence from childhood and imprisonment in the bosom of an extraordinary family to manhood and independence. Such Odysseys of youth are not uncommon; and by this time the crudities of the American scene are so familiar that the strange squalid-extravagant life of the Gant family in the hill town of Altamont, here described in profuse detail, will hold no particular surprise; what is amazing is the pressure under which this narrative is shot forth. To use a homely American metaphor, it might be called a "gusher"; for Mr. Wolfe's words come spouting up with all the force of a subterranean flood now at last breaking through the overlying strata of repression. Such native force is rare in England now; and it is impossible to regard this unstinting output of magnificent, raw vigour without a thrill and a hope that it will

From the *Times Literary Supplement,* No. 1486, July 24, 1930, p. 608. Reproduced from *The Times Literary Supplement* by permission of Times Newspapers Limited.

be channelled to great art. The present book is not great art; but its promise and its power are so extraordinary that we dwell upon them rather than upon the details of the story.

Whether or not the family life of the Gants—the Bacchic flaming father everlastingly at odds with the tight-lipped avaricious mother nursing her secret pain in dumbness, the worthless Steve, the thwarted secretive Ben, the cheery "go-getter" Luke, and the passionately serving Helen — was Mr. Wolfe's own or no, there can be no doubt that he is Eugene, the last born, who saw the light while Gant the father was booming eloquent curses outside the bedroom door, and who grew up with the taints of the Gant and Pentland blood in his body, and in his soul the sensuality, the aimlessness of his mother's family and the ache for wandering, the almost demoniac power of fantasy and sense of being a stranger in an alien world which stamped his drunken but gigantically moulded father. It is the story of a boy's escape from a thralldom to which his own nature as much as circumstances subjected him. His mother's avarice, it is true, keeps him in the low boarding house that she, though rich in real property, keeps penuriously, forces him to sell newspapers at dawn before going to school, cuts short his schooldays and sends him to the state university too soon. But it is the influence of the blood which makes him return again and again willingly to that home of strife and discomfort, bound together by its very hatreds, until its fibres are at last rent apart by the death from pneumonia of Ben — a passage of remarkable power — while Gant curses, Eliza purses her tight lips and the others wrangle hideously round the dying man. The words of Ben's last moment give a measure of Mr. Wolfe's power over words when shaken, as he is often shaken, by a spasm of emotion: —

> Suddenly, marvellously, as if his resurrection and rebirth had come upon him, Ben drew upon the air in a long and powerful respiration; his grey eyes opened. Filled with a terrible vision of all life in the one moment, he seemed to rise forward bodilessly from his pillows without support—a flame, a light, a glory—joined at length in death to the dark spirit who had brooded upon each footstep of his lonely adventure on earth; and, casting the fierce sword of his glance with utter and final comprehension upon the room haunted with its grey pageantry of cheap loves and dull consciences and on all those uncertain mummers of waste and confusion fading now from the bright window of his eyes, he passed instantly, scornful and unafraid, as he had lived, into the shades of death.

This is not merely an eloquent passage, it is summary and judgment of what has been fairly set out with intense vividness before.

This intensity of apprehension, whether sensuous or imaginative, is Eugene's mark in the novel, as it is Mr. Wolfe's in the performance. We do not need the catalogues, remarkable in themselves, of the books on which Eugene fed his voracious fancy or the rich foods on which the elder Gant, in the great days, gorged his sons and daughters; Mr. Wolfe reveals himself as one who has fed upon the honeydew and everything else under the sun. And his most astonishing passages, crammed though they are with clangorous echoes of English poetry and prose, too often falling into sheer metre, come when in contemplation of his past, he sends out a cry of lyrical agony for lost beauty. One might take to pieces the paragraph on spring that begins: "Yes, and in that month when Proserpine comes back and Ceres' dead heart rekindles, when all the woods are a tender smoky blur, and birds no bigger than a budding leaf dart through the singing trees"; or that other beginning: "In the cruel volcano of the boy's mind, the little brier moths of his idolatry wavered in to their strange marriage and were consumed"; one might trace the echoes and point out the faults, but the Marlowesque energy and beauty of them has already made such work vain. What is going to be done with this great talent, so hard, so sensual, so unsentimental, so easily comprehending and describing every sordidness of the flesh and spirit, so proudly rising to the heights? Knowing the times and the temptations of the times, we may well watch its fresh emergence with anxiety: for if Mr. Wolfe can be wasted, there is no hope for to-day.

Floyd C. Watkins

Save in His Own Country

The sudden appearance of the corpse of William Shakespeare on Asheville's Pack Square, left there by his resurrected townsmen from Stratford who had murdered him for portraying Stratfordians as clowns in the plays, would hardly have caused more excitement in Asheville than did the appearance of *Look Homeward, Angel* in the bookstores. Although there had been a few complimentary notices about the coming publication of a first novel by a local boy, no one was prepared for the events to come. Moldy skeletons had been taken from closets and hung on the tall monument in the middle of the square.

There had been novelists in the town before. Olive Tilford Dargan, poet, dramatist, and novelist, had been living in western North Carolina for years and in West Asheville since 1925. In 1920, James Hay had written a mystery novel, *"No Clue!"*, and its reception in the newspapers had been such an ironic foreshadowing of the problems with Wolfe that the long-forgotten account demands com-

From *Thomas Wolfe's Characters: Portraits from Life,* by Floyd C. Watkins. Copyright © 1957 by the University of Oklahoma Press. Reprinted by permission of the University of Oklahoma Press and Floyd C. Watkins.

parison. A local columnist created a mountain character named "Colonel Blank Babers," who commented on the novel, and he was amazed at his first encounter with fiction. After discovering "to his vast surprise" that the events and people were imaginary, the Colonel declared his opposition to fiction: " 'I never knowd they was sech doin's a gwyne on,' said the Colonel to the crowd which gathered around him on the square. 'Folks a printin' books which they aint nary word er truth in 'em. I 'spects mebbe they order be a leggislater law agin sech like they aint a lot er laws which they orter be. . . . ' "[1] And the Colonel's puzzlement raised the problem that has plagued Ashevillians and Wolfe's critics ever since: The Colonel was told by the bookseller that the characters in the novel "don't live nowheres. He says he jest made up all them things outen his head . . . they allers told me ef you see sunthin' in a book hit's bound fer to be so, an' now ef I reads a book I can't nowise tell ef hit's so er aint so." If the author of this jest had been responsible for Tom Wolfe's decision to write a book that was "so," he would have been the object of his neighbors' wrath in 1929.

What Wolfe thought the town expected of a novelist may be seen in his entirely fictitious account in *You Can't Go Home Again* of the story printed in the local newspaper about the forthcoming book by George Webber. Webber's statement to a reporter that the book is about a family in Old Catawba becomes the headline "LOCAL BOY WRITES ROMANCE OF THE OLD SOUTH." The inspired reporter expects Webber (and therefore Wolfe) to record "that stirring period of Old Catawba's past [which] has never before been accorded its rightful place of honor in the annals of Southern literature," and he inaccurately quotes Webber as hoping to "commemorate the life, history, and development of Western Catawba in a series of poetic legends comparable to those with which the poet Longfellow commemorated the life of the Acadians and the folklore of the New England countryside."[2] Despite such romantic delusions of grandeur, North Carolina's past was recorded, although not quite in the way expected by the fictitious reporter.

The jolting and shocking reviews of the novel in North Carolina newspapers presented an utter contrast to whatever glorious hopes the people had had for Wolfe's first novel. Ashevillians were not so deluded, unfortunately for Wolfe, as the critic for the *Boston Evening Transcript* who thought that the narrative was set in Penn-

---

[1] *Asheville Citizen,* February 14, 1921.
[2] *You Can't Go Home Again,* 124.

sylvania! At least they knew beyond any doubt whatsoever the setting in time, place, and people. The *Asheville Citizen*, the more dignified and detached of the two local papers, tried to remain objective and to see the novel as an outsider would. "Life burns," the reviewer ironically and perhaps naïvely remarked, "with the deep colors of human emotions and richly marked characters."[3] The description of the use of fact in the novel was embedded in a critical account of "a genius' combination of reality, which will not shrink from even the most sordid details of everyday life, and of a child-like expression of the most delightful fantasy."

Walter S. Adams' review in the *Asheville Times* was more realistic and perhaps more willing to agitate. He commented that Wolfe had written the *Angel*, "sparing nothing and shielding nothing." If Wolfe had described the town, he had also described himself, and the reviewer eagerly attacked the self-portrait: "His life here, as he boldly sketches it, was crowded with pain, bitterness and ugliness." Because of the "frankness and detail rarely ever seen in print" and the reviewer's belief that "virtually all the characters are residents of this city," he predicted that the townsfolk would be "shocked into chills" and "severely annoyed," that some would "snicker and laugh" at this "autobiography of an Asheville boy." Although Adams admitted that "the outlander" might find "unquestioned literary merit," although he himself praised the "portraiture," "narrative," and "style," he ended his attack by charging that Wolfe had "dragged forth into the light . . . any scandal" that previously had "enjoyed only a subterranean circulation."[4] When Wolfe read this review, he called it "unfairly personal," although the review in the *Citizen* had been, he thought, "splendid."[5] Refuting the *Times*, he wrote his mother that every major character revealed "a heroic spirit" in a crisis, that the family should not "be greatly concerned with what spiteful and petty people in small towns think."[6]

Perhaps the most vituperative review was published in a paper outside Asheville. Writing in the Raleigh *News and Observer*, Jonathan Daniels used the headline to charge that Wolfe had turned his fury upon the South and his native state. Thomas Wolfe, he said, had "gone the way of rebels"; there was a "reign of terror of

[3] *Asheville Citizen,* October 20, 1929.
[4] *Asheville Times,* October 27, 1929.
[5] *Thomas Wolfe's Letters to His Mother,* edited by John Skally Terry (New York, Charles Scribner's Sons, 1943), 188. (Hereafter referred to as *Letters to His Mother.*)
[6] *Ibid.,* 191.

his talent." "In 'Look Homeward, Angel,' North Carolina, and the South are spat upon." Coming from a fellow student and college friend, that statement must have hurt the sensitive young novelist, who had convinced himself that he had drawn a portrait of love. Perhaps this is one of the statements Wolfe had in mind when he wrote in *You Can't Go Home Again,* "They leveled against him the most withering charge they could think of, and said he was 'not Southern.' "[7]

If there was any love in the book, Daniels did not see it: "Against the Victorian morality and the Bourbon aristocracy of the South," he argued, "he has turned in all his fury and the result is not a book that will please the South in general and North Carolina in particular." The optimistic note of the review was the hope that Wolfe was getting "this little score paid off to his own country" and that he would be able to proceed to another work "in greater serenity of spirit." Even the lyricism was in Daniels' opinion very bad: "It is a book written in a poetic realism, the poetry of dissolution and decay, of life rotting from the womb, of death full of lush fecundity." Then he speculated on the cause of this expectoration and vengeance, settling on the family as the source of the bitterness: "Seeing any section through the Gant family," he believed, "would be like looking upon that section through the barred windows of a madhouse." The family too had been drawn in bitterness, and the result in the novel was "a life stirred only by the raw lusts for food and drink and sex and property." Of them all, he wrote, only Ben was "drawn with tenderness and feeling." As a foil to the madhouse of the lustful Gants, there was the lustful community, and here Daniels believed that a catalog of the characters would best serve his purposes, and he listed "prostitutes, white and black; loose women, Negroes and dope-fiends, drunken doctors, tuberculars, newsboys and teachers." The book was too strong a wine; Daniels found too much "blood and sex and cruelty." Finally, there was the charge of excessive use of fact in fiction. The account in the *Angel* of the University of North Carolina, as Daniels remembered the university, was "almost pure reporting."

Ashevillians did not need to be told by reviewers how to react to this book. They saw their sins as well as their virtues recorded in print, and on the first reaction all the poetry did not alleviate the luridness of the descriptions of their previously hidden errors. *Look Homeward, Angel* was so vividly true and factual that people rec-

---

[7] *You Can't Go Home Again,* 337.

ognized themselves and their neighbors; descriptions of the townspeople were so clear that a reader either discovered real sins he did
not know about or believed as fact fictitious sins that his neighbor
had not committed. The latter, of course, caused more bitterness.
Discussions of the book intruded into almost every imaginable kind
of gathering in the community, into club programs, garden club
parties, card games, and bank directors' meetings. Wolfe's sister,
Mrs. Mabel Wheaton, was shocked and deeply hurt because she
was so obviously ignored when she attended one of her clubs. People
bought copies because they had heard that they were described,
sent copies to friends whose portraits they had recognized. A defen-
sive and harassed bookseller declared to a reporter that he was
selling the novel "as a piece of literature and not as 'smut.' " After
a week of furious gossip, the *Asheville Times* called the reaction of
the town "sensational and tremendous."[8]

The bookstores soon sold out all the copies that were immediately
available, and lending libraries enjoyed for a time an unequaled
boom. "I had thought there might be a hundred people in that town
who would read the book," Wolfe wrote in *The Story of a Novel*,
"but if there were a hundred outside of the negro population, the
blind, and the positively illiterate who did not read it, I do not know
where they are."[9] Shocked by the growing scandal, the public library
stood aside from the melee, and Wolfe's college play, *The Return of
Buck Gavin*, was the only one of his writings that a patron could
borrow until Scott Fitzgerald, angered because he did not find *Look
Homeward, Angel* on the shelves six years after its publication,
stalked out to a store and bought two copies, which he plunked
down on the desk as a gift to the library. Impressed by a novel as
perhaps they had never been before, ministers preached sermons
on the subject.

Wolfe received anonymous letters, which he described in fiction,
letters, and *The Story of a Novel*. They reviled, cursed, and threatened. There was a letter that threatened to kill him, and perhaps
the post card he describes in *You Can't Go Home Again* is a literal
quotation: "We'll kill you if you ever come back here. You know
who."[10] There was another letter from an old lady who said she
would not try to prevent a mob of lynchers from dragging Wolfe's
"big overgroan karkus" through the streets.[11] When George Webber

---

8 *Asheville Times,* October 27, 1929.
9 *The Story of a Novel,* 18.
10 *You Can't Go Home Again,* 336.
11 *The Story of a Novel,* 18-19.

gets a similar letter in *You Can't Go Home Again,* the lady refers to his "monkyfied karkus."[12] There were also other kinds of reactions. In *The Marble Man's Wife,* Mrs. Julia Wolfe remarks on Cash Gudger's joy that he was in the book, and she quotes Dr. Arthur C. Ambler, who thought, "It's queer he didn't put me in the book."[13]

When there is much laying bare of human souls and their sins, weaknesses, and agonies, there must also inevitably be pathos, yet there is little indication that Wolfe had tried to ease much of the heartache. Some Ashevillians who were described have built up systems to explain their portraits in the *Angel* to themselves and to their acquaintances. One old gentleman whom Wolfe loved but whom he nevertheless presented unfavorably in the book insists over and over, even to strangers, that "Tom didn't mean what he wrote about me. He didn't mean it. He didn't mean it." Perhaps he did not intend it, but Ashevillians thought he did, and that was the tragedy. Another insists that Wolfe had to have a villain, that he was chosen for that dubious role with his own consent, and that Wolfe even let him pick his own name, which he chose from *The Virginians.* Defense mechanisms such as these belie Edward C. Aswell's contention that the reaction to *Look Homeward, Angel* was due to Wolfe's laying bare "certain spiritual realities in American life."[14]

Surely no man has been so vulnerable to suits for libel and defamation of character; surely no town has ever felt itself so defamed and libeled. Strangely, however, despite all the opportunities, no Ashevillian has ever brought a suit for libel against Wolfe and the *Angel.* Indeed, although he continued throughout all his books to use factual and, sometimes, scandalous material, there has been only one libel suit against any of his works, and that was brought against "No Door," a short story set in the North and one of the most innocuous and innocent of all his works. This suit for one hundred and twenty-five thousand dollars, furthermore, was settled out of court by Scribner's, not because they feared losing it, but because it was so upsetting to Wolfe.[15] With sentiment against him as it was in 1929 and 1930, any one of a dozen persons — and perhaps more — could have sued and collected from him and

---

[12] *You Can't Go Home Again,* 336.
[13] Hayden Norwood, *The Marble Man's Wife* (New York, Charles Scribner's Sons, 1947), 119.
[14] Edward C. Aswell, "An Introduction to Thomas Wolfe," in Walser (ed.), *The Enigma of Thomas Wolfe,* 104; also printed in the *Saturday Review of Literature,* Vol. XXXI, No. 48 (November 27, 1948).
[15] Perkins, *Editor to Author,* 118. Another legal case involved threats of libel suits. See *Letters to His Mother,* 318-25.

Scribner's. Apparently many reasons account for his escaping this harassment: the love and respect for the Wolfe family and Wolfe himself must have been one significant factor; those who knew him and had some appreciation for his writing must have escaped temptation; finally, anyone who sued would have had to face notoriety and the publication of the real facts in Asheville and elsewhere. In this instance a suit for libel would have been an admission of infamy. No one sued.

While the battle was raging in Asheville, Wolfe himself, as the reader of *You Can't Go Home Again* knows, was spending his time alternating between shrinking from conflict and furiously hurling himself at his attackers. In this last novel he tells of a reporter's interviewing George Webber, who read the newspaper and then "sat down and wrote a scathing letter to the paper, but when he had finished he tore it up."[16] Like many other incidents in the novels, this one is based on reality; but like Wolfe's other letters and papers, this one was never torn up. Written between April and September, 1929, before the novel was even published, the letter begins with thanks "for your friendly and courteous invitation to contribute an article to your columns answering critics of my book, 'O, Lost.' " He declines because "the artist is neither a debater nor a propagandist. . . . If the Asheville critics of my work infer from this that I am anxious to avoid controversy, they are certainly right. But if, as I gather from several letters in your columns, they believe that my book is a 'bitter attack' against the town, the state, the South, they are certainly wrong."[17] He had known the storm was coming, but he had failed to grasp its magnitude and violence.

In the letters, *The Story of a Novel*, and *You Can't Go Home Again*, Wolfe recorded all the variety of emotions that beset him after he heard what his friends at home thought of his book. One chapter of the life of George Webber is given to a description of the emotional crises he experiences after his home town's violent reception of his first novel, *Home to Our Mountains*. That this account is autobiographical is seen from Wolfe's description of himself in *The Story of a Novel* as "spending my time consuming myself with anger, grief, and useless passion about the reception the book had had in my native town . . . ," and again he spoke of himself at this time as "absorbed in the emotional vortex which my first book had created. . . ."[18]

[16] *You Can't Go Home Again*, 124.
[17] *The Letters of Thomas Wolfe*, edited by Elizabeth Nowell (New York, Charles Scribner's Sons, 1956), 176. (Hereafter referred to as *Letters*.)
[18] *The Story of a Novel*, 25-26.

These were the calmer admissions after several years had eroded the ugliest places from his memory. In November of 1929, he had written his mother during the time of his own bitterness. He had expected, he quarreled, "as much kindness and fairness in the town of my birth as I would get from strangers," and he was "not grateful to people who try to make of my book a diary of family and town history."[19] At that early time he was still denying the literal use of the town in fiction and contending that pain and distress were not caused by the book, but by "a misunderstanding of the book's purpose."[20]

A substantial portion of Asheville's objections perhaps came from a naïve and honest objection to Wolfe's supposed poor taste in offenses against morality, and this sort of protest reinforced the cries of those who had been described. It was the old story of provincial and puritanical mores being offended by novels because they described fictitious sins. If an Ashevillian had written Defoe's *Moll Flanders*, the reactions would have been somewhat the same, although less intense. Here was at least one manifestation of what Wolfe struggled against in his own family and community when he was trying to become a writer. Anonymous letters of protest about the immorality of *Look Homeward, Angel* were written some years after its publication.

There had been material and financial crises in the collective lives of the pioneers who had struggled to build first houses and then palatial tourist resorts in the rugged mountains. Asheville had already undergone the terrible evils of a land boom and bust second only to the great Florida boom of the twenties, and just ahead there were the trials of the Great Depression and the bank failures and scandals that were worse than in most places. The greatest trial of all, however, was the publication of a novel, ordinarily a mild and transient event that may be significant only to the author. If the columnist's Colonel Blank Babers lived until 1929, he must often have yearned for books that were entirely fiction. Always, too, in the depths of the communal mind there was an even greater fear. The pen had not been stilled and the giant had not fallen. What would Thomas Wolfe write in his next history of the town? Even the reporters sometimes feared to speculate.

---

[19] *Letters to His Mother,* 189.
[20] *Ibid.,* 190.

Advertisement of the English publisher in the *London Times Literary Supplement*, July 24, 1930.

Heinemann's advertisement, *Times Literary Supplement,* No. 1486, July 24, 1930, p. 598. Reprinted by permission of William Heinemann Ltd.

From Sinclair Lewis's Press Conference on Winning The Nobel Prize

. . .

Sinclair Lewis will not reject the Nobel Prize, as he did the Pulitzer Prize in 1926. This he made clear yesterday afternoon in an interview with representatives of the press of his country and Europe at the offices of his publishers, Harcourt, Brace & Co. He will accept the award, he said, because it is "an international prize with no strings tied."

. . .

"The Pulitzer Prize, on the other hand, is cramped by the provision of Mr. Pulitzer's will that the prize shall be given 'for the American novel published during the year which shall best present the wholesome atmosphere of American life and the highest standard of American manners and manhood.' This suggests not actual literary merit but an obedience to whatever code of good form may chance to be popular at the moment.

From Sinclair Lewis's press conference of November 5, 1930, as reported by the *New York Times*. Reprinted by permission of the Estate of Sinclair Lewis, Paul Gitlin, Administrator.

"As a result of this the Pulitzer Prize has been given to some merely mediocre novels along with other admirable novels. It is sufficient criticism of the prize to say that in the last few years it has not been awarded to Cabell's 'Jurgen,' Dreiser's 'An American Tragedy,' Hemingway's 'A Farewell to Arms,' Wolfe's 'Look Homeward, Angel,' or Cather's 'A Lost Lady.'

Mr. Lewis said that he would go to Stockholm with Mrs. Lewis to receive the prize, which he understood would be presented on Dec. 10.

The American writer to whom he paid the highest tribute was Thomas Wolfe, a young author who has written only one novel, "Look Homeward, Angel." If Mr. Wolfe keeps up the standard which he has set in this work he "may have a chance to be the greatest American writer," Mr. Lewis asserted.

"In fact, I don't see why he should not be one of the greatest world writers. His first book is so deep and spacious that it deals with the whole of life."

. . .

Sinclair Lewis

From "The American Fear of Literature"

(Address by Sinclair Lewis, December 12, 1930, on receiving the Nobel Prize in Literature)

". . . there is Thomas Wolfe, a child of, I believe, thirty or younger, whose one and only novel, *Look Homeward, Angel*, is worthy to be compared with the best in our literary production, a Gargantuan creature with great gusto of life. . . ."

From *The Man From Main Street: Selected Essays and Other Writings, 1904-1950*, edited by Harry E. Maule and Melville H. Cane. Copyright © 1953 by Random House, Inc. Reprinted by perimssion of Random House and the Estate of Sinclair Lewis.

2. Critical Appraisal: The Novel as a Whole

C. Hugh Holman

The Loneliness at the Core

Thomas Wolfe's *Look Homeward, Angel* fell on critically evil days, and they have taken their toll of its reputation, if not of its steadily increasing number of readers. It was published the month of the 1929 stock market crash, lived the first decade of its existence in the sociological and Marxist-minded thirties, and presented to politically sensitive critics a hero of whom its author approvingly wrote: "... he did not care under what form of government he lived —Republican, Democrat, Tory, Socialist, or Bolshevist. ... He did not want to reform the world, or to make it a better place to live in." That hero, Eugene Gant, was hardly in tune with the intellectual temper of his times.

It is a frankly autobiographical book, "a story of the buried life," written by a man who, by his own confession, "failed to finish a single book of . . . [Henry] James." Yet its whole existence has been during a time when the technical and formal considerations of Henry James have triumphantly established themselves as the

From *The New Republic,* CXXXIII (October 10, 1955), 16-17. Reprinted by permission of *The New Republic,* © 1955, Harrison-Blaine of New Jersey, Inc. and C. Hugh Holman.

proper criteria for fiction. For a book largely devoid of the traditional fictional or dramatic structure, almost naïvely innocent of "crucial plot," and seemingly dedicated to the lyrical expression of emotion not very tranquilly recollected, the age of Jamesian criticism has proved patronizingly hostile.

As Herbert Muller, by no means an unfriendly critic of Wolfe, has said:

> His limitations may be exposed most clearly on his own ground, by setting his novels beside such other autobiographical novels as *Sons and Lovers, Of Human Bondage, The Portrait of the Artist as a Young Man* and *Remembrance of Things Past.* In these the hero is a creation, not a *nom de plume,* and his life a work of art, not a flood of memories. In this company Wolfe appears a very artless young man.

In such a context of critical opinion it has required effort to maintain a serious attitude toward Wolfe and his first book, *Look Homeward, Angel,* which is almost universally acknowledged to be his best novel—effort that few serious critics have made.

I believe that my experience is fairly typical. I belong to the generation that read *Look Homeward, Angel* when it was new and they were very young. It wove for me an evocative spell as complete as any book ever has. It seemed to me that this was not a book; it was life and life as I knew it. I brought to it, a very young book, the naïve and uncritical response of the very young. Such an attitude did not survive, and in a very few years I became aware of the irresponsibility, the rhetorical excess, and the formless confusion of the book.

To go back to *Look Homeward, Angel* in 1955 and seriously to read it has been an experience in some ways as startling as the initial reading was, and it has made me aware that it is a different book from what I had thought and a much better one.

The standard view of *Look Homeward, Angel* has assumed one of three attitudes: that literal autobiography very thinly disguised constitutes the important portion of the book; that what form it has was given it by the editor Maxwell Perkins rather than its author; and that the book is most interesting in terms of Wolfe's acknowledged and pervasive debt to James Joyce.

The first attitude has resulted in a mass of biographical data, but, as Louis D. Rubin has recently pointed out, the value of the book must ultimately be determined in terms of its quality as *novel* rather than its accuracy as personal history. The second attitude reached the epitome of critical severity with Bernard DeVoto's "Genius is not Enough," and Wolfe is today generally credited with the major, if not the sole part in determining the form of his first two books.

The debt to Joyce, although everywhere obvious, seems to me almost nowhere truly significant. The least admirable portions of *Look Homeward, Angel* are those very portions where the ghost of *Ulysses* hovers visibly on the sidelines—portions such as the well-known record of the schoolboys' trip home from school, with its ironic pattern of mixed quotation so reminiscent of Joyce.

I think the first thing that strikes the mature reader who goes back to *Look Homeward, Angel* is the realization that it is a book enriched by a wealth of humor and saved from mawkishness by a pervasive comic spirit. This quality of the book is usually lost on its young readers, because the young very seldom see much amusing in themselves. Yet everywhere in this book one is aware that it is a very young book, not because its attitudes are themselves very young, but because it is a record of the inner and outer life of a very young boy.

The author looks back at youth with longing and love, but also with a steady but tolerant amusement. This is nowhere more apparent than in the hyperbolically presented day-dreams of "Bruce-Eugene" and in the very youthful posturing of the college student so earnestly set upon dramatizing himself. The humor is itself sometimes very poor and very seldom of the highest order. It is satire directed with crude bluntness; it is hyperbole lacking in finesse; it is *reductio ad absurdum* without philosophical seriousness. Wolfe is not a great comic writer, but his comic sense gives distance and depth to his picture of his youthful self.

For all its rhetorical exclamation about emotion, *Look Homeward, Angel* is a book firmly fixed in a sharply realized and realistically presented social environment. The book comes to us almost entirely through Eugene Gant's perceptions, but what he perceives is very often Altamont and Pulpit Hill (Asheville and Chapel Hill, N. C.) and he perceives them with a wealth of accurate detail. At this stage of his career, Thomas Wolfe had few serious pronouncements to make about man as a social animal (in his later career he was to attempt to make many), but he had a realist's view of his world.

It is a view colored, too, by a broadly Agrarian attitude, however much he was contemptuous of the Agrarians as a group. His picture of Altamont is a picture of a place mad with money and size, of a people submerging everything of value in valueless wealth. This view, the sword on which Eliza Gant is first hoist and then eviscerated, extends from the family to the life of the town and finally to the imagery of the whole book. As an example (and it is but one of hundreds), when he hears his idol-brother Ben talking sententious businessman nonsense, "Eugene writhed to hear this fierce condor prattle this stale hash of the canny millionaires, like any obedient parrot in a teller's cage."

Further, we perceive as a rediscovery that beneath the extravagant rhetoric, the badly and baldly rhythmic passages—the ones that eager young men reprint as bad free verse—there is a truly lyric quality in Wolfe's writing. With an abnormally keen memory for sensory perceptions, what Wolfe called his "more than ordinary . . . power to evoke and bring back the odors, sounds, colors, shapes, and feel of things with concrete vividness," he is able to bring to bear vicariously on our five senses the precise content of a given scene and to make it poignantly and palpably real.

And here he works, not as a rhetorician asking us to imagine an emotion, but as an imagist rubbing "the thing" against our exposed nerve ends and thereby calling forth the feeling. It is, perhaps, in this ability to use authentically "the thing" to evoke emotion that the finest aspect of Wolfe's very uneven talent appears.

A new look at *Look Homeward, Angel* shows us that it is a book, not only of Eugene's "buried life," but one about tragic loneliness. Few lonelier pictures exist than the ones here that show the insularity within which Eliza and W. O. Gant live. This W. O. Gant, a rich and hungry man in spirit, who was never called by his wife Eliza anything except "Mr. Gant," strove by rhetoric, invective, alcohol, and lust to make somehow an impress on the unresponsive world around him. He is the ultimate tragic center of a book which deals with spiritual isolation almost everywhere.

Certainly the book lacks formal novelistic structure. If its core, as I believe, is W. O. Gant, then it contains a wealth of unresolved irrelevancy. If its central pattern is somehow linked up with brother Ben, as Wolfe seems to feel that it is, then we must regretfully assert that Brother Ben is a failure, the only really dead person in a book noteworthy for the vitality of its characters.

Yet *Look Homeward, Angel* has a consistency and an integrity of its own. In a way different from those indicated above, it presents a world. And as we survey that world and its characteristics, it begins to appear very much like the universe of that surprisingly modern eighteenth century figure, Laurence Sterne; and the thought impresses itself upon us that Thomas Wolfe has created for Eugene Gant a Shandean world and that his book has something of the inspired illogic of the universe of Walter Shandy and Uncle Toby.

Both *Look Homeward, Angel* and *Tristram Shandy* defy formal analysis. Both are concerned with the education of the very young. Both see that education as essentially the product of the impact of the world outside upon the young mind. Both describe that education through memories in maturity. And both gain a certain quality of detachment through the comic or amused presentation of material, although Sterne's humor is better than Wolfe's and more pervasively a portion of his book.

Both Eugene and Tristram are the products of mismatched parents, both pairs of whom exist in their eternally separate worlds. Both heroes have older brothers who die; both are given to rhetorical excesses; both have a tendency toward unsatisfied concupiscence; and both embarrass us by "snickering," as Thackeray pointed out about Sterne. But these are superficial similarities; more real ones exist in method, language, and theme.

Look Homeward, Angel and *Tristram Shandy* are both ostensibly about their heroes, are records of these heroes' "life and opinions," yet neither Eugene nor Tristram is as real as other characters in their books. Uncle Toby, "My Father," and to a certain extent "My Mother" dominate *Tristram Shandy* and overshadow its narrator-hero. W. O. Gant, Eliza Gant, and Helen Gant dominate *Look Homeward, Angel,* and beside them the viewpoint character, Eugene, pales into comparative unreality. Furthermore, both books are family novels, peculiarly rich in brilliantly realized, hyperbolically presented familial portraits.

Both Wolfe and Sterne were adept at the precise, fact-laden description in which the thing evokes the feeling. Both were given to the representation of emotional excess in terms of heightened sensibility. Sterne is famous for this characteristic; in Wolfe, one needs only to look at the Laura James sequence to see the "novel of sensibility" present with us again.

Both men were remarkably proficient at capturing the individual cadences of human speech and reproducing them with sharp accuracy, and both delighted in the rhetorically extravagant; so that their works present, not a unified style, but a medley of styles.

But most significantly of all, both Wolfe and Sterne were oppressed with the tragic sense of human insularity, with the ineffable loneliness at the core of all human life. Walter Shandy sought a word to communicate with wife and brother, and he sought in vain. His wife walked in inarticulate silence beside him. Eugene Gant was striving for "a stone, a leaf, an unfound door." W. O. Gant, with all his exuberance and overbrimming life, remained "Mr. Gant" to a wife who never understood "save in incommunicable gleams."

And the whole problem of life, loneliness, and memory with which in their different ways these two books are concerned is for both writers bound up in the mystery of time and memory. Uncle Toby and Tristram, as well as Sterne, brood amusingly and seriously about kinds of time. For Wolfe and his hero, Time is the great unanswerable mystery and villain of life.

The world of Eugene Gant is a Shandean world. And in that inconsistent, unbalanced, illogical, incongruous, incomplete, and lonely universe, the secret of *Look Homeward, Angel's* sprawling formlessness, its unevenness, and its passages of colossal failure and of splendid success exist.

Unless we demand that all novels be neat and concise, *Look Homeward, Angel* has much to offer us still: a clear, detailed picture of a town; two extravagantly drawn but very living people, Eliza and W. O. Gant; a comic sense that lends aesthetic distance; a poignantly lyrical expression of the physical world of youth; and a picture of the individual's incommunicable loneliness.

Francis E. Skipp

The Editing of
Look Homeward, Angel

Thomas Wolfe first met Maxwell Perkins, the senior editor at Charles Scribner's Sons, on 2 Jan. 1929. They met to discuss the manuscript of Wolfe's first novel which he then intended to call *O, Lost!* and which was to be published as *Look Homeward, Angel* in the following October. Perkins' good manners and simple elegance made an immediate impression on the sensitive provincial, but it was the editor's grasp of a manuscript which Wolfe had despaired of publishing that caught Wolfe's enthusiasm. He wrote to his preparatory school teacher and devoted admirer, Margaret Roberts, that "For the first time in my life I was getting criticism I could really use. The scenes he wanted cut were invariably the least essential and the least interesting; all the scenes I had thought too coarse, vulgar, profane, or obscene for publication he forbade me to touch save for a word or two."[1]

Five days later, on January 7, the two met again. Since their first meeting Wolfe had set down in a pocket notebook proposals for revi-

From *The Papers of the Bibliographical Society of America,* LVII (First Quarter 1963), 1-13. Reprinted by permission of The Bibliographical Society of America and Francis E. Skipp.
[1] *The Letters of Thomas Wolfe,* ed. Elizabeth Nowell (New York, 1957), p. 169.

sion probably growing out of Perkins' analysis of the manuscript. In that notebook, which Wolfe kept during December 1928 and January 1929 are these entries:

Notes

I propose to correct and revise the mss 100 pages at a time, and if possible to deliver 100 pages every week.

Proposal for Condensation

First, to cut out of every page every word that is not essential to the meaning of the writing—If I can find even 10 words in every page this wd = 10,000 or more in entire mss. Then, to cut out the introductory part and write a new beginning. To shorten the child-in-the-cradle scenes. To shorten St. Louis scene save for Grover's death. To correct all unnecessary coarseness in language, and to cut out unnecessary pages and passages scattered through the book—To revise Newport scenes and to omit scene with woman on the boat—To shorten State University part as much as possible—and further, in the university scenes, to keep Eugene's relation with the family uppermost.

Questions

What about several pages that list all the smells and odors?—What about child's fantasies?

—What about the seduction scene with the waitress in Charleston?

What about paper-boy scenes, and especially that one with negress?

Scribner's suggests unity of scene as far as possible—What about Julia's [Eliza's] various trips to Hot Springs, Florida, New Orleans, and so on?

Propose to Scribner's

If I can get some definite assurance of their willingness to publish the book—if revised—I will set to work immediately.

The first thing I will do will be to write new introduction & omit the present beginning. I can have this ready and delivered one week from the present interview.[2]

Apparently agreeing that Wolfe should proceed in the manner proposed, Perkins conceded with a smile that it would be all right, as Wolfe put it, to "say something definite to a very dear friend"—undoubtedly Aline Bernstein—but with Yankee caution he would say

---

[2] "Pocket Notebook 8 (December, 1928–January, 1929)," in the Thomas Wolfe Collection of William B. Wisdom at the Houghton Library, Harvard; catalog number *46AM-7(69).

only "that their minds were practically made up." The poet John Hall Wheelock, Perkins' subordinate, was less canny. As Wolfe was leaving the editorial floor, John Wheelock took his hand and said, "I hope you have a good place to work in—you have a big job ahead." Wheelock's open-heartedness removed Wolfe's lingering doubt. He rushed out to Fifth Avenue, as he himself said, "drunk with glory."[3]

Wolfe—and Perkins too, as it turned out—did have a big job ahead, but how big, actually, was it? Dozens of literary anecdotes turn upon the extraordinary size of the *O, Lost!* typescript. The publisher William M. Sloane recalled in the 3 Dec. 1938 *Saturday Review of Literature* that the typescript came to Longmans, Green when he was a young reader there. It was, Sloane said (page 4) "a block of typewriten pages so big it measured about two feet vertically and had to be tied in a number of packets." When the novel was rejected, Sloane added, "we sent the manuscript back, presumably in a truck." Melville Cane, the lawyer and poet, told in the 22 Sept. 1951, *New Yorker* how Wolfe had brought him the manuscript in two suitcases and after five nights spent in reading a small fraction of it Cane told Wolfe (page 26) "that while it showed enormous talent, no publisher would take the trouble to edit it." Cane went on to recall that Maxwell Perkins did undertake the chore "and when it appeared Tom sent me a copy with a letter saying I couldn't be expected to read every page, but would I please read every other page? A very nice letter, under the circumstances."

As a matter of sober fact, the typescript which had begun the rounds of the New York publishing houses in the spring of 1928 was 1,114 pages long, standing the height of two and a quarter reams of paper or about five inches.[4] It contained approximately 330,000 words. With its acceptance by Scribner's in January 1929 at last a certainty, Wolfe began the task of reducing it to a publishable length. By the following August, with the book in page proof, he could summarize the whole process in a letter to an old friend, George W. McCoy of the *Asheville Citizen.* Wolfe wrote:

> When they accepted my book the publishers told me to get busy with my little hatchet and carve off some 100,000 words. . . . I did get busy, and in a month or two had cut twenty or thirty thousand words, and added fifty thousand more. The editors then felt it was time to intervene: they restrained me, and helped me in every way

---

[3] Wolfe described this scene to Margaret Roberts. See *Letters,* p. 170.
[4] "Typescript of the First Form of *Look Homeward, Angel*" (carbon copy of the unedited typescript), Wisdom Collection, *45M-156F.

with criticism, editing, and a vast amount of patient, careful work. They have been magnificent—I have not time or space to tell you how fine they have been—and now we have a book which can be read without demanding a six month's leave of absence.[5]

The good humor that is unmistakable here, the pride in achievement, and the generous recognition of the help Scribner's had given him conceal the anguish Wolfe had experienced during the long editorial task that stretched itself out over six months. Signs of rebellion are to be seen in an entry he made in the pocket notebook he kept during February and March, 1929, where he wrote:

On "the passion for Condensation"

It may be a very bad passion. Probably what we need is a passion for expansion. What most of us mean when we say we have a passion for condensation is simply that we haven't much to write about. Perhaps The Bridge of San Luis Rey is a better book than Of Human Bondage, but it is certainly not a better book simply because it is shorter. If the story of San Luis Rey can be told in 200 pages well and good. But that does not mean that all stories should be cut to 200 pages. As a matter of fact the long novel can easily hold its own against the short one even if we attempt to choose the best novels written during the century. It seems to me that most of them would be long ones. To name a few.—

Jean Cristophe	The Olde Wives Tale
Of Human Bondage	Buddenbrooks
Ulysses	The Magic Mountain
Sons and Lovers	The World's Illusion
	An American Tragedy[6]

And it was at this time that Wolfe confessed to his agent, Madeleine Boyd, "I am at work on the book, but it is a stiff, perplexing job. I stare for hours at the manuscript before cutting out a few sentences: sometimes I want to rip in blindly and slash, but unless I knew *where* the result would be disastrous."[7]

The work was still going on in May and getting no easier. "I am working every day with the editor of Scribner's, Mr. Perkins, on the revision of my book," Wolfe wrote to his sister, Mabel Wheaton. "We are cutting out big chunks, and my heart bleeds to see it go, but it's die dog or eat the hatchet." Conceding that unity was being gained

---

[5] *Letters,* pp. 199-200.
[6] "Pocket Notebook 9 (February, March, 1929)," Wisdom Collection, *46AM-7(69).
[7] *Letters,* p. 175.

at the cost of some material he thought good, Wolfe added, "This man Perkins is a fine fellow and perhaps the best publishing editor in America. I have great confidence in him and I usually yield to his judgment."[8]

In short, Wolfe's experience in attempting to cut the typescript of *Look Homeward, Angel* to publishable size and to give it more formal unity was proving conclusively something he had long suspected—that he could not, reliably and consistently, distinguish between the superfluous and the essential. This inability, in the last analysis, was an inability to discern within his work what inherent form it possessed. He could see, as a practical matter, the desirability of reducing his typescript to a size that made its publication and sale easier, but to accomplish the task he had to rely heavily upon the judgment of his editors. This necessary reliance had two consequences, first, an extravagant admiration for an editorial talent he himself lacked and second, resentment against the editor who advised the cutting of material which often seemed to Wolfe to be as worthy of publication as that which was allowed to remain. Maxwell Perkins himself was later to reminisce about the editing. Perkins wrote:

> The extent of cutting in that book has somehow come to be greatly exaggerated. Really, it was more a matter of reorganization. For instance, Tom had that wonderful episode when Gant came back from his far wandering and rode in early morning on the trolley car. . . . This was immediately followed by an episode of a similar kind where Eugene, with his friends, walked home from school through the town of Asheville. . . . By putting these episodes next to each other the effect of each was diminished, and I think we gave both much greater value by separating them.[9]

Perkins to the contrary, the problem was mainly a matter of cutting and not of reorganization. The 330,000 word typescript was reduced by a net amount of about 90,000 words. To accomplish this, 147 cuts were made which eliminated a little over 7,900 lines or roughly 95,000 words. And mainly to suture the resulting discontinuities, sixteen passages totaling 408 lines or about 5,000 words were added. Only one transposition of importance was made. The narrative of Gant's early morning homecoming from his far-wandering in the West was lifted out of a long Joycean passage (not from beside the home-from-school passage) and moved back in time

---

[8] *Ibid.,* p. 177.
[9] "Thomas Wolfe," *Harvard Library Bulletin* I (Autumn, 1947), 272.

to a logical position in Chapter VII. The remainder, the celebrated "night scene," retained its place and appears as Chapter XIV.

Unfortunately, the typescript of *Look Homeward, Angel* in the William B. Wisdom Collection at Harvard's Houghton Library is an unedited carbon copy. Since its pages are unmarked by the editor's pencil they hold no clues to the identity of the person who made the cuts, cuts which are to be discovered only by collating typescript and text. Nor is there evidence either in a typescript or a manuscript to establish positively the authorship of the sixteen passages added. The testimony of Wolfe's letters already quoted, however, suggests that the cuts were made mainly by Maxwell Perkins with Wolfe's acquiescence. The bridging passages were undoubtedly written by Wolfe himself, for he worked closely with his editors until the book was in page proof. Furthermore, the scheduled date of publication was comfortably met, a circumstance which rules out the liklihood of emergency repairs by a second hand. And finally, other Wolfe typescripts preserved at Harvard—especially the typescript of *Of Time and the River*—bear eloquent testimony that while almost all the cuts were made by Perkins, all the words (with interesting but most minor exceptions) were written by Wolfe.

Why was the typescript of *Look Homeward, Angel* cut nearly thirty per cent? To be sure, a novel of 330,000 words is a bulky book and expensive to produce, but Scribner's in the depths of the Great Depression was to publish *Of Time and the River*, a book considerably longer. The Wolfe of 1929 was indeed an unknown upon whom Charles Scribner would be less inclined to gamble than the Wolfe of 1935, but if all of *Look Homeward, Angel* had seemed to the firm to be of equal literary merit and of equal relevancy to the central narrative, the House of Scribner would very probably have published it in all its great length. An analysis of the material cut, however, suggests that the typescript was cut for sufficient literary reasons, and that speculation upon whether or not cuts were made from considerations of publishing expediency are essentially irrelevant. These cuts, listed as categories and arranged in the order of their extent, are as follows:

1. Material lying outside the central narrative: 29 cuts, 3,267 lines
2. Disproportionate development: 26 cuts, 2,566 lines
3. Ineffective material (inappropriate, banal, or mannered): 21 cuts, 755 lines
4. Impropriety: 25 cuts, 524 lines
5. Disproportionate development of character (a special case of 2 above): 14 cuts, 516 lines

6. Authorial comment: 22 cuts, 442 lines
7. Non-dramatic characterization: 5 cuts, 97 lines
8. Material dangling as the result of an antecedent cut: 3 cuts, 44 lines
9. Repetition: 2 cuts, 13 lines

Easily the largest cut was that of the typescript's first 1,377 lines, or the first fifty typescript leaves with a deep run-on onto the fifty-first. This section told of the migration of Gilbert Gaunt from England to America where his gipsy and improvident spirit settled at last among the Pennsylvania Dutch, and of the youth and young manhood of one of his children, Oliver Gant, until Oliver in his westward drifting reached Altamont. The narrative is interesting although the impression it gives of living experience is less forceful than that of the remainder of the novel because it was not drawn from Wolfe's own life. But even here there was excellence. The scene in which young Oliver and his brother watch a division of Lee's army march along a Pennsylvania road on its way to Gettysburg was to be used as a reminiscence of the dying Gant in *Of Time and the River*. The novel, however, is "A Story of the Buried Life," of Eugene Gant and not of his father, Oliver, however important Oliver may be. The introductory narrative in its great length is clearly too little relevant to the central theme to have been retained as it stood. The first three pages of the published novel (to paragraph four on page 5) are a condensation, about 1,400 words long, written to supplant what originally extended to more than 16,500 words.

Another substantial cut falling within this first category was one of 364 lines, the material on typescript leaves 172-84 and immediately preceding Chapter XII of the published novel. This section concerned Pett Pentland, a sister-in-law of Eliza Gant and a most minor character. It told of Pett's exploitation, under the guise of charity, of an orphan taken into the Pentland home. It was a penetrating and well-told story but clearly outside the novel's scope and irrelevant to its central theme.[10]

---

[10] Irrelevancy was ample justification for this cut, but Wolfe might have had second thoughts about the possibly libelous character of the tale, if not in 1929, at least in 1935 with Asheville's fury over the novel still fresh in his mind. In the spring of 1935 Elizabeth Nowell, Wolfe's literary agent, had written from New York of finding among Wolfe's manuscripts four narratives she considered to be possibly saleable as short stories. Wolfe replied from London in a letter postmarked 23 April 1935, "I don't know where the hell you *found* the four stories — if one of them is about Pett and the orphan girl for god's sake try to change the names or the locale if possible." (Autograph letter signed, Wisdom Collection, *46AM-14.)

The most extensive cutting of material disproportionately developed, the second category, was done among the many episodes Wolfe supplied on Eugene Gant's life at the state university. This portion of the novel takes Eugene away from Asheville and the interaction between Eugene and his family which gives the novel what unity and balance it has. Consequently, the fifty-five pages in the published novel devoted to Eugene's college days, although absorbing and undeniably involved with the development of the novel's central figure, seem at the same time to be at least partially a digression. This section, however, is but two-thirds as long as Wolfe wrote it. A total of 915 lines on Eugene's university life was cut.

The inappropriate can be discriminated from the irrelevant sufficiently to justify its inclusion with the banal and the mannered as a related literary fault in category three. One such inappropriate episode of ninety-eight lines was cut from among the night scenes of Chapter xiv. This episode, which is to be found on leaves 269-72, is spirited and hilarious, sharply written and well controlled, a satire on the very wealthy who were building great estates near Asheville. In it the handsome daughter of a retired English Jew mounts her fiery horse with such ardor and manages him with such authority, that her departure from the stable-yard leaves the grooms erotically aroused and expressing their aspirations in wild pantomime. As an episode, however, it is too fanciful, too facetious, too much at a variance with the rest of the night scene chapter to have been kept.

Another such cut has intrinsic interest as a fair parody of T. S. Eliot, echoing "Sweeney Among the Nightingales" and "Burbank With a Baedeker, Bleistein With a Cigar." Had the parody stood, however, it could not have failed to offend as an abrupt shift in method destroying the unity of effect of Wolfe's montage of impressions in his night scene chapter. As a further comment on the material which appears in the novel as the last paragraph on page 184 and the first paragraph on page 185, Wolfe had written on leaves 268-69:

Mose Extinct

Defunctive music in the dim
Drugged thickets of the convolutions,
A flying gleam leaps to the rim,
Mose stirs, and thinks of quick ablutions.

Too late: the slack jaws open wide,
The sloping thighs resist and quiver,
The hasp slides through, the walls divide,
Red chasms to a crimson river.

The lids rip open at the seams,
The fat brain dreams but reads its error.
Buttered on steel the moonlight gleams,
The balls are strung on steel and terror.

Cloud charioted up the silver beach
The Thracian huntress rolls the disk.
Jeff, keeping loot and loan in reach,
Shelves round the haunch of Molly Fiske.

All day the hungry housecats whine,
The flies grow drunk with blood and loathing,
Day bleeds to death, and Mr. Stein
Puts tickets on the underclothing.

Although the obscenities and improprieties which Wolfe was so touchingly willing to eliminate from his typescript yielded only 524 lines, the twenty-five separate cuts under this fourth category are the second greatest number made. These cuts seem to be about equally divided between those justified by material of questionable taste or of psychological falseness and those where an overly nice editorial conscience took from the novel something rich though earthly, or forced the revision of an episode that consequently became less genuine.

An example of the former is the child Eugene's recollection of the smell "of a fizzing and sulphuric fart, bottled in the warm sheets; . . . and of cloven ponderous cheeses like toe jam," a recollection cut from leaf 84. The uncut remainder appears along with a catalogue of remembered smells as paragraph three, page 85, of the novel. On leaves 337-39, Eugene's description of the wig worn by John Dorsey Leonard, the proprietor-master of "The Altamont Fitting School" was derisive and cruel, ugly and without charity. Its thirty-five lines were cut and replaced by the single transitional line appearing just before the break on page 225 of the novel.

Leaves 871-75 were given over to a psychologically false episode in which Eugene, filling a college vacation in wartime with work on the Norfolk docks, encounters in an Italian ship's stateroom the mistress of the first officer. The narrative of this encounter is an adolescent fantasy tricked out with such manifestations of passion as shoulder-biting and ending when Eugene "spent his force upon her proud body in one annihilating shaft of fire."

On the other hand, the sensibility which detected in instances like these the offensive, the inhumane, or the false also allowed an over-niceness of taste to cast out what well might have been allowed to remain. In Chapter IV the consciousness of the infant Eugene is given as a forecast and a pattern for the tragi-comedy of man's life. The tension between these two elements of our existence is present throughout this section (in the novel, pages 36-44). For this reason it would seem that line four on page 37 where Eugene's "lack of coordination of the centres of control, the undisciplined and rowdy bladder" is described would have been better as Wolfe first wrote it on leaf 29—"the undisciplined and rowdy bladder jetting in the midst of tranquility, its unsuspected stream." And when Eugene has his first sexual experience, the episode as it is given in the novel (pages 410-11) terminates in his impotence. In the unedited typescript Eugene does indeed embrace Lily Jones, the Exeter prostitute, but mechanically. His disillusionment is even more utter and complete. The excised episode is more credible and convincing.

The failure to maintain proportion between a character's importance in the narrative and the space given over to his characterization (category 5) is a special case of disproportionate development (category 2). In writing *Look Homeward, Angel,* however, Wolfe was carried away by his interest in a number of his characters simply for their own sake. To be sure, the 104 lines devoted to the character of Henry Pentland on leaves 64-68 would seem to be warranted by his extraordinary personality. Wolfe subsequently was to change Henry's name and paint him, full figure, in "A Portrait of Bascom Hawke," a Scribner's Prize Novelette which was to be sliced into sections and fitted into Wolfe's second novel, *Of Time and the River* where Henry Pentland, now Bascom Pentland, is a major character. Henry Pentland, however, had no place in *Look Homeward, Angel.* The half-dozen words at the foot of page 13 that identify him as a member of the Pentland clan are all that remained after the typescript was cut.

Similarly, Wolfe's interest in the sinister character of Judge Webster Tayloe (Sondley in the typescript) extended the portion of the night-scene chapter which concerned the judge to four times the length at which it now stands in the novel (pages 181-83). Leaves 257-63, the material cut, continue the excellent, somewhat Faulkneresque, analysis of a type of now-vanished southerner, but the continuation exceeds due proportion.

On twenty-two occasions Wolfe could not resist stepping to the footlights to address his audience directly. On many of these occasions his appearance was a fleeting one, but it was remarked by his editor nonetheless, and excised. In the last paragraph on page 118 Wolfe tells how Gant, with craft and dishonesty, led Eugene to renounce the pony which rashly had been promised as a Christmas present. Leaf 140 of the typescript ends the vignette with the branding of Gant's action as "the crippling dull insensitiveness of the parental tradition." In the editing, Wolfe's authorial comment (category 6) was detected and cut. The paragraph, which runs over to page 119, now ends with the phrase, "the crippling dull deceit."

Elsewhere, Wolfe came forward with more of a flourish. Leaf 99 of the typescript ended what was to be the novel's Chapter VIII, but it contained this postscript, with its Steinian conclusion:

> Meanwhile, Julia [Eliza] had begun to dream of Dixieland. Ah, but we could tell you more if we would. But not yet, not yet. The time is not ripe. But it will come! Suspense! Suspense! Suspense!
> Julia had meanwhile begun, she had begun meanwhile, she meanwhile had begun to dream of Dixieland.

This mannered intrusion had no place in a novel whose unifying consciousness was that of a child developing into young manhood. Nor was it appropriate that when Eugene's fear of venereal infection collapsed with the diagnosis of crab lice Wolfe should seize the moment to philosophize. Reflecting upon those moments in life when we expect confirmation of our fears, Wolfe observed:

> Before we come to that hedge we can fancy nothing beyond but ruin, or curative death: after we pass it, we find the broad lands of a richer world. And we pass it—some of us—again and again, losing something priceless and irrecoverable, gaining a world and new music, stranger, profounder, and sadder than any we have known. And our lives widen out, not infinitely, but immeasurably, like great circles on a shoreless pond, until the sudden cry of knowledge is strangled in our throats by death.

This mixture of metaphor is to be found on leaf 693 where it completed the paragraph which appears after the first break on the novel's page 417.

The remaining three categories under which cuts were made—non-dramatic characterization, material dangling as the result of an antecedent cut, and repetition—do not warrant analysis and example, since one is an accidental effect and the other two responsible for only 110 lines between them.

There was, then, reason for cutting 95,000 words from Thomas Wolfe's 330,000 word typescript, *O, Lost!* The analysis of these cuts suggests that the disproportion, which in one sense or another most of them represent, came about because Wolfe seemed to feel that he had to tell all that his prodigious memory could recall about his fore-bears, his family, and himself. Years later Maxwell Perkins was to confide to James Jones, "I remember the horror with which I realized when working with Thomas Wolfe on his manuscript of 'The Angel,' that all these people were almost completely real, that the book was literally autobiographical."[11]

But if Wolfe's method of laying end-to-end the transmuted but insufficiently discriminated facts of his life made his typescripts an ill-proportioned novel it had one fortunate result: it gave the novel an underlying unity, the unity of one life in evolution, and consequently it gave the novel structure and form. Except for the single transposition of Gant's homecoming from the night-scene chapter to an earlier and more logical place in the narrative, the form of the published novel was present in the typescript before it ever was read by a publisher.

---

[11] *Editor to Author, The Letters of Maxwell E. Perkins,* ed. John Hall Wheelock (New York, 1950), p. 296.

Maxwell Geismar

Diary of a Provincial

'All serious work,' Wolfe says in the preface to his first novel, 'is autobiographical,' but with him more than conventionally so, his work is his life. When he attempted in 'The Web and the Rock' to write a more 'objective' novel, the Webber hero becomes progressively more and more Wolfian, and by the last sections the novel almost abandons the attempt at anonymity. In the recounting of his life, moreover, we are fortunate that Wolfe had few false reticences. The artist, as Somerset Maugham has noticed so nicely in 'Cakes and Ale,' is the only free man. The treachery of friends, the departure of his beloved, the unaccountable malice of acquaintances— these are the grist of the writer's mill. Whatever blows life deals him, he alone can repay them with profit to his soul, and often indeed to his pocketbook. And if through his writing Wolfe did not always gain this complete artist's freedom (which, by the way, has its ambiguous aspects for the beloved, the friend, and even the acquaintance) he at least achieved a wonderful frankness. Nothing was to

From *Writers in Crisis: The American Novel Between Two Wars,* by Maxwell Geismar. Copyright © 1942 by Houghton Mifflin Company. Reprinted by permission of Houghton Mifflin and Maxwell Geismar.

Wolfe, but writing made it more so. His novels are the dairy, tremendous, often inchoate and very possibly unique in our time, of the artist in America. And more particularly of the writer in our provincial America. Here, indeed, is the local origin of Wolfe's 'unspeakable and incommunicable prison,' the Pentlands of Wolfe's first novel, in which, enchained, his broken angel looks vainly homeward.

In the old myth, as we know, man himself, as the broken angel, has his memories of an earlier heaven before his fall. We remember Milton's paradise, with its modest claim of

> things unattempted yet in prose or rhyme

—or Eve's garden itself. With our more analytic modern sense we have come to see that the haunting feeling of man's better past derives in part at least from the peace of the womb in the individual's life, and that perhaps of sheer inanimate matter in the race's memory of its existence. How strong a theme this is in our history! So cruelly pointing backward to its ultimate goal of death, and perhaps even so ironically the hidden and despairing cause of all our infinite progress. We find many traces and currents of the theme in European literature, from Plato to the Wordsworthian infant trailing his clouds of glory. And too few traces of it are found in American culture, where this idyllic garden is never in the forsaken and haunting past, but, as we all know, immediately ahead of us: paradise and prosperity right around the corner. No melancholy mysticisms for our pragmatic optimists in a land where work, not recollection, will prove our salvation.

Wolfe is perhaps the only major modern author who has seized upon the theme of the lost paradise for his first novel, and he had his reasons. If we for the moment ignore the soaring rhetoric which marks 'Look Homeward, Angel,' we may see in it a very realistic portrait of Wolfe's society. Out of its calculations and pretensions Wolfe has fashioned a sort of heroic scene. But the calculations and pretensions remain. He embellishes the provincial rudeness with poetry, but the ornamentation also accentuates the frame. It is Gant, of course, with his memories of rich meadows, corn, plum trees, and ripe grain, of the old rich pioneer America, who is the exile in the Reconstruction South. It is Gant who recalls the 'great, forgotten language, the lost lane-end into Heaven.' Why here? O Lost! Lost indeed the Gantian South with its gray and withered Altamonts, its squalid Toytown cities, the 'pasteboard pebbledash' hotels. The muddy clay roads. The slattern people. The rows of yokels strung like apes along the fences. The drunken McGuires (the more talented souls of Wolfe's South are the drunkards) and the Pentland dwellers. But is there only the southern idiocy to oppose Gant's northern madness? The Pentlands, Wolfe says, by marriage and intermarriage among their own kin, 'could boast of some connections with the great, of some insanity, and a modicum of idiocy'—for once a Wolfian understatement. For Bacchus Pentland, Armageddon was due any day now, and for his family, as a matter of fact, it seems to have arrived. We remember the first reception of Gant by the Pentland clan, this tribe 'who saw one another only in times of death, pestilence and terror.' The males with their birdlike winks and nods, the children with their lapping idiot grins, the roaring of the wind outside, 'remote and demented.' Was it a time of joy for the northern Gant, his marriage with the daughter of this clan? It proved in fact a time of death, pestilence, and terror, for it marked his union with them, the prelude to his long and painful conquest by them.

And for the young Eugene of the novel, these Pentlands are the South with variations. There are two characters who stand out in some contrast: the younger brother Ben, whom Wolfe tries unsuccessfully to create as a tragic and lovable person, and the teacher, Margaret Leonard, who is perhaps the only character in the book possessing a genuine warmth. And here, of course, we come upon the major fault of 'Look Homeward, Angel.' The writer who is fully himself is certainly the rebel. His nature, his obligation, his essence is the civilizing spirit which evaluates and condemns. In the midst of Utopia the writer, as it were, must protest the divine injustices, and in the context of, as yet, an imperfect and mortal society, he must remain continually sensitive to human abuses. He is at once society's irritant and antiseptic. Yet to become wholly this, to lose the sense of loyalty to one's origins, of devotion to one's land or of faith in one's neighbors, to lose this basic sense of a creative if always skeptical affection for his material, is for the writer and his society equally sterile. The most brilliant satire which has no focus within our human hopes leaves us its victims, perhaps, but not its followers. The writer who in his intelligence forsakes his humanity—an Aldous Huxley, for example, in the manner of 'After Many a Summer Dies the Swan'—loses his own purpose as a writer.

It is incorrect to mention Huxley and Wolfe together here, and only as the extreme may illustrate the mean. For Wolfe's entire struggle, as we shall see, becomes the attempt to remedy the emotional deficiencies he felt within himself. But in the range of his first novel, which always arouses our interest, the moments which also compel our sympathy are few. With all Wolfe's marvelous faculty of characterization, he omits the essential of our identification with these people of 'Look Homeward, Angel.' We see them brilliantly and we hardly feel them at all. We are the outsiders watching a variety of human specimens operating in their milieu, which should be ours. We recognize Wolfe's Altamont, but we are bound to it by few ties of affection, nor those of mere companionship, common neighborliness, nor by any mutual concern for our collective achievement. We exist in it merely, as it were, by proximity. Just so, Wolfe was born in the South, but he shared with it little except the accident of birth. A strange irony, and one which we must return to later, that this writer—so American in his temperament, so filled with the necessity of his belonging to his land in order to fulfill his destiny— should be denied the ordinary heritage of a home, of a place and people to love.

Yet what was there in Wolfe's early life to evoke this obvious loving-kindness, this ordinary and basic attribute of art, the common identification of a writer with his brothers, which the critic is almost ashamed to identify, such is our period, and must speak of with bated breath? If Margaret Leonard is the one person in Wolfe's portrait of his youth who gives out some humanity, who has some interest in Wolfe's hero, Eugene, can we say as much for her fellow teachers? 'What is an Epode, Mr. Leonard?' asks Eugene's friend of the drawling, stupid schoolmaster. 'Why,' said Mr. Leonard reflectively, 'it's a form of poetry.' 'Hell,' said the boy, 'I knew that before I paid tuition.' Is there very much in fact which these boys didn't know before they came to school? The dry and distorted forms of Cicero, Ovid, Lucretius, which John Leonard presented to his adolescent audience, squirming in its seats, projecting petty obscenities to divert itself from such intolerable boredom—what connection have these 'classics' with Eugene's actual life? Nor was Leonard an unusually stupid man, Wolfe tells us. He was indeed

> an example of that sad liberalism of the village — an advanced thinker among the Methodists, a bearer of the torch at noon, an apologist for the toleration of ideas that have been established for fifty years.

The ludicrous Shakespearian pageant, one of the finest scenes in 'Look Homeward, Angel,' and in which Wolfe shows very sharply the satiric gift which was later to constitute his most impressive achievement, is the logical symbol of the false values of Eugene's education. And just so Wolfe himself sums up his impression of the more enlightened thinking of the 'university':

> The appraisal of personality, like all other appraisal with them was coarse and blunt. They were suspicious of all eminence. . . . The vast champaign of the world stretched out its limitless wonder, but few were seduced away from the fortress of the State, few ever heard the distant reverberation of an idea. They could get no greater glory for themselves than a seat in the Senate, and the way to glory —the way to all power, highness and distinction whatsoever—was through the law, a string tie, and a hat.

Such is the verdict of our hero upon his total provincial education. It is harsh, biased, no doubt, but there is reason for its bias. Even Margaret Leonard, who encourages at least Eugene's avid hunger for knowledge, though without much discipline or discrimination in the sort of knowledge, has perhaps little sense of Eugene's real needs. His hunger is also for human relationships as well as poetry, for some knowledge also of his own physical and mental development, this hero tormented by his family's disgrace and by his own adolescent sexual fantasies. 'She was an inspired sentimentalist,' Wolfe writes of Margaret Leonard. 'She thought she "knew boys" '—

> In fact, however, she had little knowledge of them. She would have been stricken with horror if she could have known the wild confusion of adolescence, the sexual nightmares of puberty, the grief, the fear, the shame in which a boy broods over the dark world of his desire. She did not know that every boy, caged in from confession by his fear, is to himself a monster.

Yet the 'fear' which cages in Eugene is not at all a necessary condition of a boy's education except within the strait limits of the provincial-puritan view of youth. From the insistence, indeed, with which these 'sexual nightmares' intrude upon Eugene's life, it might almost seem that his education had in the end only one major function: the stimulation of his prurience. But if Eugene's formal education cannot thus be viewed as highly constructive, what can be said of his sexual education itself?

Only, I am afraid, that it was compounded, in a pattern familiar to our society, of secrecy and salaciousness, and of ignorance which is no bliss. The colored prostitute, Ella Corpening, with her pathetic Kewpie dolls and calendars from the Altamont Coal Company, her moaning, undulating, writhing 'Jelly Roll,' is in fact an advance for the young Eugene, at least from the classroom obscenities, the sneaking sexualism of his white companions; for Ella's passion, if commercial, is also honest. The little waitress, Louise, may add something further to Eugene's amorous sophistication, but hardly to his sense that often a human relationship may accompany the sexual one. From Louise, the young Eugene moves to Lily Jones in her house in Exerter, Lily Jones with her 'coy and frigid modesty' —

> She yielded her kisses with the coy and frigid modesty of the provincial harlot, turning her mouth away. . . . She chafed him with rough, embarrassed professionalism. In a moment she rose impatiently. 'Let's git started,' she said. 'Where's my money?'

Is the pursuing of such affection, then, the lost language Wolfe seeks, the lane-end into paradise? If love should be the core of the adolescent's growth, is this to be the love which rewards him? In Eugene, Wolfe writes, the ghost turned grievously away. 'The lost bright wonder died.' Based on such premises how can Eugene's final affair with Laura James, the climax of 'Look Homeward, Angel,' if it attempts to be idyllic, have any genuine substance? It seems, despite all of Wolfe's efforts, artificial and empty; so too is the young Eugene in respect to any previous knowledge of a sound relationship. It is literary, and D. H. Lawrence; what other standard can Eugene create for himself? Certainly not that of reality. And if in it the pornographic again often replaces the passionate, this has been the essence of Eugene's sexual education.

Love like charity begins at home. Of course, Eugene's family should have created the emotional security which might compensate for the terrors of these other areas of his learning, but it is among the members of his family that we find the greatest indifference toward the facts. It is precisely this family, indeed, which contributes most to the sense of shame, fear, disturbance underlying Eugene's youth. Eliza, Eugene's mother, we recall, since her husband is a tombstone cutter, declares that death is not remunerative. 'People,' she thought, 'died too slowly.' With Eliza's entrance into real-estate speculation, she gains 'a freedom she had never known.' But this 'freedom' is that of materialist America, of Lardner's U.S.A., the freedom of possession and power which in the end is only a superior sort of bondage. What does Eliza not offer up as human sacrifice to this insensate freedom?—her husband, her children, her home, and, of course, herself. A Rockefeller is reputed, in Matthew Josephson's 'Robber Barons,' to have stated the classic American dictum of family life: that he cheated his sons every chance he could. 'I want to make 'em sharp. I trade with the boys and skin 'em and I just beat 'em every time I can. I want to make 'em sharp.' But to Wolfe's Eliza we cannot even attribute this rather primitive parental concern. Tending her property, she could not also tend to her children. Hoarding old string, empty cans, paper, anything she may retail at a profit, symbol of the property psychology which a Balzac flayed in France, she is the twentieth-century version of Shakespeare's 'snapper-up of unconsidered trifles.' Sometimes she attains a comic dignity, grandly ascribing to her tubercular clients 'a little bronchial trouble.' But lacking at last any warmth and ease of personality, we feel only her increasing sterility, a woman who lusts only for money. We share with Eugene his gradually perceptive hatred, first of Eliza's effect on her husband Gant, and then on the boy Eugene himself:

> He felt, rather than understood, the waste, the confusion, the blind cruelty of their lives . . . the conviction that their lives could not be more hopelessly distorted, wrenched, mutilated and perverted away from all simple comfort, repose, happiness, if they had set themselves deliberately to tangle the skein, twist the pattern. . . . He saw plainly by this time that their poverty, the threat of the poorhouse, the lurid references to the pauper's grave belonged to the insensate mythology of hoarding.

And the growing perception of the actual conditions of his existence, the young Eugene materializes a little later in a perhaps less rhetorical but more convincing statement to Eliza on Gant's dying agonies:

> My God, my God, where are we going? What's it all about? He's dying—can't you see it? Don't you know it? Look at his life. Look at yours. No light, no love, no comfort—nothing. . . . Mama, mama, in God's name what is it? What do you want? Are you going to strangle and drown us all? Don't you own enough? Do you want more string? Do you want more bottles? . . . Do you want the town? What is it?

As though, indeed, all the young men of America were crying such phrases to certain other industrial Lords of Creation!

Such, then, are the outlines of 'the buried life' from which a Thomas Wolfe slowly and painfully extricated his spirit. If we are accused of simplifying the picture Wolfe gives us, it is simply because the grim outlines are softened by the lyric passages of 'Look Homeward, Angel.' It is precisely this other strain in his first novel which we must now for a moment examine. The rich meadows, corn, plum trees, the ripe grain Gant forever mourns, and for the splendors of which, now forever lost, he may only substitute the tides of his preposterous rhetoric, a richness of words for the vanished richness of fact—this is Gant's memory of a different America. And Wolfe's long, rich elaborations of food throughout this book and his later novels also, the orgies of tremendous feeding, the hunger for richness not only of food, but of personality, action, knowledge, sensation, of words and life itself—these are Wolfe's desire. Memory and desire: what power resides in these attributes of the human temperament, and especially when they are denied their realization by the facts of our life! Then indeed they rise triumphant to their extremes, and their excesses, just when they are most evidently betrayed by the realities of our existence, to demonstrate beyond doubt the dominance of the wish over the statistic. Wolfe's passion for the sensuous wealth of life, his repeated invocations to black, wet, spermy earth, existence oozing, bursting, with fertility—

> huge, frosty apples, whole hogs, smoked bacons, great bins full of flour, dark, recessed shelves groaning with preserved cherries, peaches, plums, quinces, apples, pears . . .

— we must surely establish this as not the truth of his own life, but its hunger; and a hunger based exactly on the material and spiritual poverty of the life he describes in such harsh and condemnatory terms. The excesses of Wolfe's quest for abundance are in short attributable to its absence in his early environment.

We must mention in this respect Wolfe's affinity (which was surely a southern sacrilege) for the Jews of his novels, an affinity which was to lead him to such strange terminating conditions of his life. Like him the Jews are the outcasts of society, the exiles, the strangers. But they often seem also to possess the very qualities denied to Wolfe by his own existence: laughter, ease, a generosity of temperament. Thus the ridiculous and ironic excesses of gaiety and warmth with which Wolfe later endows his New York Jewish friends, and which to a large degree led to catastrophe when Wolfe was faced with facts rather than his romantic and wishful imagination. For the Jews are, as Dorothy Parker noted, just like everybody else, only more so, and even they could not measure up to Wolfe's exorbitant demands. In the meantime, Wolfe was to preserve his special affection for them, those Jewish students of his, as he tells us in 'The Story of a Novel,' who stood first even in the accusing circle of his dreams of guilt; the little Jews of 'Of Time and the River,' with their swarthy faces, sensuous beings, full of the life and laughter lacking in Wolfe's own. And they also are, as Wolfe is, alone, imprisoned. Like him, alas, they also sought their lost, forgotten language, their lane-end into paradise, strove to escape the unspeakable and incommunicable prison of this earth.

A prison indeed if we may trust Wolfe's portrait of his youth. Early, if somewhat absurdly, echoing Wordsworth's omniscient infant, he saw himself as the sad one, 'caged in that little round of skull, imprisoned in that beating and most scared heart,' his life forever walking down lonely passages —

> He understood that men were forever strangers to one another, that no one ever comes really to know any one, that imprisoned in the dark womb of our mother, we come to life without having seen her face, that we are given to her arms a stranger, and that, caught in the insoluble prison of being, we escape it never, no matter what arms may clasp us, what mouth may kiss us, what heart may warm us.

And if this is perhaps a little prescient for the baby, it is certainly evident to the mature Eugene.

Is it likewise so evident to all the rest of us, the common condition of our existence, the inexorable terms of our own being? If the dominant theme of imprisonment, which is the framework of 'Look Homeward, Angel,' certainly is to a large extent the immutable analysis of our worldly activity, it is just as certainly true that the characteristic of the human, as against the brute, spirit lies in the effort to defy it: to break the bars of our savage bondage, to escape from this brutalizing loneliness. To communicate and share, to depend on and support our fellow exiles and prisoners, to fuse through our common experience and effort a communal unity — these are the defiant aims of the progressive forces in humanity. Civilization is the attempt to escape from this prison. And long ago the poet's song reminded us

> Stone walls do not a prison make,
> Nor iron bars a cage.

But what was there in Wolfe's provincial culture to support such a faith? The instruments of our salvation from the Wolfian tomb are precisely those which, as we have seen, were denied to him: family, friends, love, and knowledge. These, like Ariadne's 'clue of silk' which rescued ancient Theseus from the labyrinth, are the slender but nevertheless sufficient thread to lead us from the domains of our own modern solitude, but for Wolfe the thread, the clue, was missing.

The pilgrimage of a Thomas Wolfe from this point onward is the attempt, often misdirected, sometimes even lacking consciousness of his problem, and yet in the end with a sure purpose, to solve this enigma for himself and his work. Meanwhile we should notice that Eugene's farewell to his Altamont has, for this prison-pent soul, a certain degree of vigor. Years later, Wolfe tells us, his hero was still afraid of his South. Even —

> when he could no longer think of the barren spiritual wilderness, the hostile and murderous entrenchment against all new life—when their cheap mythology, their legend of the charm of their manner, the aristocratic culture of their lives . . . made him writhe—when he could think of no return to their life and its swarming superstitions without weariness and horror, so great was his fear of the legend, his fear of their antagonism, that he still pretended the most fanatic devotion, excusing his Northern residence on grounds of necessity rather than desire.

But finally, Wolfe concludes, it occurred to Eugene that his education, his family, his friends, these people of the South had given him nothing —

> that neither their love nor their hatred could injure him, that he owed them nothing, and he determined that he would say so, and repay their insolence with a curse.

The 'curse' was, of course, 'Look Homeward, Angel,' but what Wolfe owed to the South was not in fact so easily concluded.

Richard Walser

Look Homeward, Angel

Usually the first book of a young writer is a book of discovery. From his meager experience, accentuated by his youth, comes a knowledge so new and so startling and so wonderful that its pain is almost beyond bearing. Mellow, many-faceted understanding is not for now; understanding is the hard reward of decades of summers. Youth's knowledge, youth's discoveries, are as sure as an April dawn.

Look Homeward, Angel was written out of a need for discovery as well as a need for assessing the knowledge of a young man. By 1926 Thomas Wolfe had found out many things, but only through a creative act could his knowledge be refined into truth. For artists, it has always been so.

Wolfe was in England that summer, at loose ends. At night he lay in his bed remembering he had been born in North Carolina and wondering why he was then in England. The writing began in the first person. Later the name "Eugene" would have to be substituted for the pronoun "I." Before the first draft was completed,

From *Thomas Wolfe: An Introduction and Interpretation,* by Richard Walser. Reprinted by permission of Holt, Rinehart, and Winston, Inc., copyright owner, and Richard Walser.

seventeen large ledgers would be filled with his generous scrawl. Creation demanded sixty cigarettes a day, twenty cups of coffee, food gulped down whenever he could manage to tear himself away from the ledgers and whenever he happened to recall he was hungry — or so Wolfe wrote of his author-hero in *You Can't Go Home Again.* The writing proceeded without any appraisal of the results, "in simpleness and nakedness of soul," he said, with a "child's innocency and wonder."

What was the book about? A month after its publication Wolfe tried to make clear to his mother that its theme was clearly stated in the opening pages: "that we are born alone — all of us who ever lived or will live — that we live alone, and die alone, and that we are strangers to one another, and never come to know one another."

That the novel is autobiographical is apparent but, then, Wolfe thought that all worthwhile fiction is autobiographical. It could be no other way, for every man is his own center and all he knows comes from his experience. But that the novel is *fact* was not true. A writer might create one character out of a hundred persons whom he had known. Fiction was, he defined, only "fact selected and understood . . . arranged and charged with purpose," and the world Wolfe created was always inside him, never outside. If the people in his book had their basis in human experience, the life and being they possessed was only what he himself gave them.

The plot of *Look Homeward, Angel* — perhaps *plan* is the better word — corresponds roughly with the first twenty years of Wolfe's life. In 1900, at the Southern mountain town of Altamont in the State of Old Catawba, Eugene Gant was born, the eighth child and the fifth son of an itinerant Pennsylvania father and a hill-born mother. The union of William Oliver Gant and Eliza Pentland Gant had, from the beginning, been a stormy one. The father was a romantic, poetry-quoting stonecutter, while the mother was primarily of a practical turn of mind. The night Eugene was born, Gant had been on a glorious drunk. As the child grew up, he along with his brothers and sisters was caught hopelessly in the crosscurrents. He knew he would always be the sad, the lost one, 'imprisoned in that beating and most secret heart." From his earliest moments of consciousness, memory folded back upon him and the "bell rang under the sea."

When not quite six, Eugene began public schooling. His brothers and sisters, who thought him "queer," had little time for him. Almost at once he learned to read, and then to write. In the first grade he still had curls which his mother could not bear to clip, and the pack of wolves at the school, sensing a stranger among them, mercilessly persecuted him. In the third grade he was writing little poems and stuffing them in his desk. As for games, he never learned to play them or to be part of a team.

At home, Eliza, grieving over the death of her son Grover at the World's Fair in St. Louis, nevertheless pushed the brothers into the street to earn money selling newspapers and magazines. W. O. continued his periodic brawls, making no secret of his frequent visits to the local brothel. Soon, Eliza opened up Dixieland, a boarding house, and with her went Eugene. His sister Helen stayed behind with her father at the old house, the other children — Daisy, Steve, Ben, and Luke — moving restlessly between the two but mainly eating at Eliza's table. Eugene hated Dixieland, was ashamed of it, and felt he had lost not only social caste and dignity but all the essence of privacy.

The duality of his life began to shape the lad. Though his mother's conduct affronted him, he recognized the kinship, even so, and shared with her the potency of memory and talk, and a "powerful clairvoyance, the wild Scotch gift." His sensory impressions developed so keenly that "at the moment of perception of a single thing, the whole background of color, warmth, odor, sound, taste established itself." His father, he admiringly thought, was not a mere maker of tombstones, but a master craftsman of enduring works which would prevent his being forgotten when he died. In the lost area between these two dominating but conflicting forces, Eugene wanted to gain the love he did not have and he wanted to be famous. These ambitions were not unlike those of all who were ever born.

The last four years of his preparatory training were spent at a private school operated by John and Margaret Leonard. John was a spiritless creature, but Margaret, upon the foundation of Eugene's love of books, brought the boy to literature. With Margaret, for the first time he was able to reveal to someone else the buried life which he lived. Not even to Ben, whom he loved above all others, could he open a window.

Just before his sixteenth birthday, Eugene entered the state university at Pulpit Hill. His first year was painful and lonely, pressed within himself as he was by a hostile world of hostile students who made fun of his strange tall figure. Thereafter he gradually managed to bear the taunts and even play up to the howlings of the merrymakers. But Wolfe does not deal minutely with Eugene's college years. Most of the chapters are anecdotal: a visit to a prostitute in a nearby town, an incident in a Latin class, and so on. What is more clearly detailed is the boy's inner life, his alternate elation and dejection, the development of a centaur-cry which tried "to unburden its overladen heart in one blast of pain and joy and passion." By the end of his senior year, Eugene had conquered the visible enemy, he had become a big man on the campus, but the gnawing from within was still there. Even at the pinnacle of campus success, Eugene sensed that his fellows, most of whom were little more than industrious, mediocre hacks, "safe, sound, and reliable," resented his brilliance.

Three episodes punctuate this section of the novel. During the first summer vacation Eugene fell in love with Laura James, a boarder at his mother's Dixieland. Without acknowledging her engagement to be married, the older girl led him into a love which was young, innocent, and beautiful, ironically blooming within a setting of drunkenness and cheap humanity. The picnic scene, concluding with the rich prose-poem "Come up into the hills, O my young love," is followed by Eugene's lonely agony at the realization of her defection.

A second episode was his journey to Norfolk to help in the national effort during the height of World War I. It was there, in a period of sweat and awkward misdirection, that he knew he could survive on his own, and more and more he sought escape from family and home town.

The third concerned the illness and death of Ben during the influenza epidemic of 1918. With the sympathetic Ben gone, Eugene felt there was no longer any reason to remain encased within the imprisoning mountains. In that final lyric chapter, he discussed with the ghost of Ben a journey out, and Ben told him that a man's world is himself. Even so, Eugene was determined to leave on the next day. He was twenty years old.

Such a bare and inadequate outline gives no hint of the opulence of *Look Homeward, Angel*. Besides Eugene, there are in the novel several characters monumental in their graphic individuality and personality. Those most unforgettable are Gant, Eliza, Ben, and Helen.

William Oliver Gant is memorable chiefly because he had a tremendous gusto for life. No passive figure, he was either violent in denunciation or ecstatic in approval. To his family, in spite of his comic vulgarity, he brought a ritual which gave a pattern to their days. The children loved him for being a good provider; he brought home whole carcasses of meat, huge baskets of farm produce; at breakfast he heaped their plates "with great slabs of fried steak, grits fried in egg, hot biscuits, jam, fried apples"; he had a love of abundance. He was lusty in his speech, covering Eliza with abuse at one moment, in the next railing aloud some Shakespearean lines in inebriated glory. He was sensual, moving from wife to wife, spawning numbers of children, assaulting Negro cooks, and indiscriminately showing himself at Queen Elizabeth's "house." Yet, though he loved his home and his brood, he was the Far-Wanderer with a nomad's hunger for voyages — the hunger that haunts all Americans, Wolfe wrote, and makes us homeless strangers. If a symbol be needed, Gant's life was like a river, the Mississippi River, "rich with its own deposited and onward-borne agglutinations, fecund with its sedimental accretions, filled exhaustlessly by life in order to be more richly itself." The thing which obstructed the flow was Eliza's Dixieland, "this damnable, this awful, this murderous and bloody Barn." There amid the chattering, gluttonous boarders he felt most alone and lost. Gant was dying slowly of cancer, but no one would tell him, and he would not give up.

The character of Eliza is more complex. The mountains of her birth gave her independence and energy and pride, plus a minstrel's flair for storing old stories away in her mind for eventual recounting. In unhurried dips into memory, she took her time, pulling into by-ways and exploring the paths of events till all was swept clean. She was egocentric without being egotistical; she was dependent on the love of her family without surrendering her native freedom. When life turned against her in the form of an unhappy, unfortunate marriage, Eliza gathered to herself other symbols of security — "old string, empty cans and bottles, paper, trash of every description." If her acquisitiveness angered her husband and children, she did not bother to explain, or perhaps she did not know, the real reasons for her frugality. The change came in her at the time when Eugene was weaned at the age of three. "Something in her stopped," Wolfe wrote; "something began." The death of Grover the following year left her, as other disappointments left the other members of her family, a lost person. From that point on, it is all too easy to blame Eliza for the disasters which followed one another — the splitting of the family, for instance, and Eugene's efforts to escape, and Ben's death — but beneath the exterior was a generous, noble woman compensating for the buffets of fortune in the only way left to her. Wolfe thought of her that way. If personal relationships had no meaning, money and property did have one. Her cross lay in her family's lack of understanding, not in any spiritual or moral weakness.

Ben, with the gray eyes, the bumpy skin, the shapely head, and the perpetual scowl, had with Eugene a kinship outside the family circle. Apparently only Ben had any knowledge of the boy's problems. This was true because he, like Eugene, was always trying "to find some entrance into life, some secret undiscovered door — a stone, a leaf — that might admit him into light and fellowship." He never found the door, but there was ever, as Wolfe puts it, the sound of the lost world and the great forgotten language. In the absence of earth-bound communication, Ben talked to his Demon. Eliza, delivering some of her practical advice, would be countered by Ben's cocking his head up to his dark angel and exclaiming, "Oh, my God. Listen to that!" As Eugene knew and observed, he spoke to his angel quickly and often. If the chapters on Ben's death have been said to be one of the great death scenes in all literature, the opinion is due in large measure to Wolfe's writing of one of the most profound experiences a young man ever had. For Eugene, it was the death of recognition.

Alongside these tragic portrayals, Wolfe drew a warm picture of Helen, unsparing, big-boned, open-hearted. She was the solid one amid the otherwise uncertain family ties, and it seemed to be a need within her to throw away her boundless energies in service for her family. She was always there when she was wanted, complaining maybe, but intensifying her efforts to negate the complaints. Helen's intense love for her father was her signal of self-denial. She could not bear to leave him in the less sympathetic hands of Eliza. She was like her father in lustiness, abundance, and raucous humor. But Helen, unlike the others, was not lost.

Daisy, Steve, and Luke, individual though they were, are less vividly presented; yet they, too, with all their strengths and weaknesses, often seem oversized and godike in a primal world. Outside the Gant family the characters shrink into everyday proportions.

Wolfe's desire was not, however, merely to write a novel telling of the pains of youth surrounded by people who either were incapable of understanding or were powerless to help. His intention was far greater, and perhaps if one is to get at this intention, he ought to look closely at the clues Wolfe has provided.

Look Homeward, Angel carries as its subtitle "A Story of the Buried Life." What did Wolfe mean by this? Evidently the phrase was borrowed from Matthew Arnold's short poem beginning "Light flows our war of mocking words," in which Arnold comments on that part of man's life hidden behind the disguises he wears and on his inability, except in moments of love, to reveal himself. This buried life, even so, is the real one, the essential one which lends meaning to existence. Wolfe extended this notion into what he called his "plan" for the book. Before the novel was accepted for publication, he wrote that in it "There are two essential movements — one outward and one downward. The outward movement describes the effort of a child, a boy, and a youth for release, freedom, and loneliness in new lands. . . . The downward movement is represented by a constant excavation into the buried life of a group of people, and describes the cyclic curve of a family's life — genesis, union, decay, and dissolution." The buried life was a secret life, and though even Gant and Eliza had such a side, it is mainly Eugene, and to a lesser degree, Ben, who are shown to be strangers to the world.

With Eugene the secret life had much to do with imagination, by means of which he daydreamed of huge ships and faraway cities and lands which opened out. In his imagination there was belief in the great virtues: tenderness and gentleness, beauty and love and goodness, valiance and glory. There were more intense moments like the one in which he lusciously imagined himself the only male in a town of pretty women whence all the men had fled, and how he would loot the shops and cellars and fulfill all his sensuous desires. There were more comical moments in which he saw himself as "Ace Gant, the falcon of the skies, with 63 Huns to his credit by his nineteenth year." And there were the more honest moments when he admitted "the wild confusion of adolescence, the sexual nightmares of puberty, the grief, the fear, the shame in which a boy broods over the dark world of his desire," when "every boy, caged in from confession by his fear, is to himself a monster."

The essence of the buried life was a continuation of prenatal existence. If Wolfe borrowed Arnold's phrase for his subtitle, he was even more influenced by the Neoplatonic romanticism of Wordsworth and Coleridge. In the prose-poem facing the first chapter are these well remembered words: "Naked and alone we came into exile. In her dark womb we did not know our mother's face; from the prison of her flesh have we come into the unspeakable and incommunicable prison of this earth." Eugene was born trailing Wordsworthian clouds of glory, but all too soon he was suspended in time, caught in life's prisonhouse, and the sound of the great bell ringing underseas was dimmer and dimmer. As time went on, the prison house became more stifling, and though he sought to escape the prison gates, he came to realize that his incarceration was complete and he found comfort in the fantasy of the buried life. Thus walled in, he projected "an acceptable counterfeit of himself which would protect him from intrusion." At birth he knew the word — "the lost key opening the prison gates, the lane-end into heaven" — but eventually, like all who are born, he forgot it.

Re-echoes of pre-existence and the buried life persist throughout the novel and give it unity. To go a step further, Albrecht contends that Wolfe utilized, besides the pre-existence-and-return myth, other Platonic contrasts: dark and light, many and one, isolation and union, imprisonment and freedom, shadow and reality. His study and love of the romantic poets left their mark.

While the subtitle and opening sentences of *Look Homeward, Angel* established a mood for the story to follow, they do not state a theme. Almost from the first days when Wolfe started writing the novel, there was no doubt in his mind what his intent would be. Though the materials would come from his own life, he planned to tell, he wrote Mrs. Roberts, "the story of a powerful creative element trying to work its way toward an essential isolation; a creative solitude; a secret life — its fierce struggles to wall this part of its life away from birth, first against the public and savage glare of an unbalanced, nervous brawling family group; later against school, society, all the barbarous invasions of the world." The words are clear. Wolfe was then twenty-five years old; his young spirit was being assailed by the world which he had sought outside his mountains; he needed at that moment for the past to be caught, as it was with Proust, through memory; and he felt the necessity to put down on paper the agony of his present problem.

The pith of any work of fiction is conflict. Eugene Gant's conflict was one between himself and world, between himself and family, school, and society. He struggled against a father whose artistic nature he thought had been wasted, against a mother whose love he believed he had lost, against brothers and sisters who had succumbed to the pressures and been defeated. Inwardly he took up arms against a home town which he felt was united to destroy him. He was determined to keep his individuality intact.

Eugene's fight is all the more difficult because he was constantly aware that, in spite of his strong resolution to preserve his self, the elements of Chance were operating full time. Eugene had only to go back in memory to know that "the loss or gain of a moment, the turn of the head, the enormous and aimless impulsion of accident, had thrust into the blazing heat of him." And so it would go on, each moment being the culmination of thousands and thousands of years. Cause led on to Cause, and Man's life was not ordered by mind and reason but was the frenzied fumbling of Chance, Variety, and Fate. If the battle was unequal, the best one could do was to isolate himself — to "wall" himself in — and "escape" into life, not from it.

Like all young men, Eugene pondered the reasons why life should be this way, but these occasions were rare. Generally they came in fancied seconds when Time was suspended and no-Time took over. Eugene would see a woman from a train window, and suddenly the train was motionless, the woman was frozen without movement, and Time was stopped. The reader of *Look Homeward, Angel* may recall that the instant after W. O. Gant had sold the angel to Queen Elizabeth, he stood upon the steps of his stonecutter's shop and the pulsing fountain in the public square was held in photographic fixity. Where was man headed? 'Where now? Where after? Where then?" There was no answer. Only death was sure.

Throughout the novel, the mood and theme are enriched by a number of symbols which must be understood if the poetic nature of the fiction is to be fully realized. A translation of poetic symbols is not always easy, and the reason is aptly given by Richard Chase in *The American Novel and Its Tradition:*

> . . . a poetic symbol not only *means* something, it *is* something— namely, an autonomous truth which has been discovered in the process by which the symbol emerged in the context of the poem. If it still permits us to think of it as an ordinary symbol—as something that stands for something else—we see that it does not point to anything easy to express. Rather, it suggests several meanings. . . . Furthermore, the "poetry" of a novel will probably reside less in the language than in the rhythm and relation of picture, scene, character, and action . . .

This is especially true of Wolfe, where the symbolic words *are* something at the same time they carry another intention. Moreover, like the whale in Melville, the intention is constantly shifting, rarely static.

A good example is the Angel of the title. Here are the lines from Milton's "Lycidas":

> Or whether thou [the poet's college friend who has drowned],
>   to our moist vows denied,

Sleep'st by the fable of Bellerus old,
Where the great Vision of the guarded mount
Looks toward Namancos and Bayona's hold.
Look homeward, Angel, now, and melt with ruth:
And, O ye dolphins, waft the hapless youth.

Here Milton invokes the protector angel St. Michael to turn from foreign threats in order to weep for a disaster at home. The same meaning may be applied to Wolfe's novel. Heaven is urged to look toward home and "melt with ruth" rather than gaze afar for tragic possibilities. Altamont and the Gant family have their own pathetic lives. This poetic interpretation of the word *angel* is balanced by a palpable image: the stone angel on the porch of Gant's shop. This angel, which Wolfe wrote was responsible for his title, "had come from Carrara in Italy, and it held a stone lily delicately in one hand. The other hand was lifted in benediction, it was poised clumsily upon the ball of one phthisic foot, and its stupid white face wore a smile of soft stone idiocy." As a youth in Baltimore, Gant had seen such an angel and had then yearned to carve a similar one and thus release evidence of the creative urge within him. He never learned to carve such an angel; the artistic impulse burned and died as the prisonhouse closed about him in the philistine confines of Altamont. In this instance, the angel is the symbol of the creativity which, though throbbing, is suppressed in most men.

A third and more compelling interpretation, and in no way unconnected with the other two, is the angel of Ben and Eugene. Wolfe generally substituted the word ghost, the ghost being the spirit from some pre-existence. "O lost, and by the wind grieved, ghost, come back again," Wolfe reiterated. The ghost is a lonely spirit. It is sometimes synonymous with the loss of innocence as when, after Eugene's first visit to a prostitute, he "was haunted by his own lost ghost: he knew it to be irrecoverable." But the angel-ghost image, like any wraith, shifts and changes. Often it stands for corporeal life, which is not real at all, but a zombie taking the place of the real. At such times the ghost wails for a return into life from exile. The ghost therefore is lost. Eugene, himself a ghost, seeks the way of returning. "The way is here, Eugene. Have you forgotten? The leaf, the rock, the wall of light. Lift up the rock, Eugene, the leaf, the stone, the unfound door. Return, return." Then, after Ben's death, Ben *becomes* Eugene's ghost, and Ben's answer to the question "Where is the world?" is the simple one "*You* are your world." In that last chapter, the dead Ben finally has life, and he is therefore no longer a ghost. The stone angels begin to move, and with them Eugene believes himself freed. The ghost-angel reappears as creative power. (See Albrecht's "Time as Unity.")

Often in the same context as the angel is the triple symbol "a stone, a leaf, a door." In *The Prelude*, Wordsworth writes of "a tree, a stone, a withered leaf," a phrasing upon which Wolfe apparently based his refrain. In his novels, the *stone* is reminiscent of Gant's angel and its metaphorical meaning for the artist; it is also the solid element in life's uncertain transformations. The *leaf* — the "withered leaf" — is, by way of contrast, consonant with decay and death. The most frequently used of the three words is the *door*, and the search for the door, which, if one could find and enter it, would mean artistic and spiritual fulfillment.

There are many other ringing words, of course. The train, with its apostrophe to America and to America's unknown people and places, sometimes becomes for Eugene the "gateway to the lost world." More than any other symbol, the train is Wolfe's signature, as the star is Robert Frost's.

And there are the mountains, which represent Eugene's bound-in life and his desire for escape.

All of these symbols are tied in with Wolfe's mood and theme, culminating in Eugene's conviction "that men do not escape from life because life is dull, but that life escapes from men because men are little."

The symbols are interwoven into the prose paragraphs, and when the reader comes upon them, they are like the soft low notes of a musical instrument, sounding to remind him that outside the story of written words is a meaning deeper and more profound than the progressive narrative before him.

Wolfe's search for America is less evident in *Look Homeward, Angel* than in the later books. In his first novel he was so concerned with an examination of his youth that he had not yet projected his subject matter very far beyond Altamont and Old Catawba. The country out there was largely *terra incognita*. Still there are hints that the stretch of America was in his mind. Gant's trip to California by train called forth a rhapsodic passage. When Eugene takes a trip down into South Carolina (by train, of course), there in the night-time beyond the windows was "the American earth — rude, immeasurable, formless, mighty."

If the quest of America was yet to come, not so Wolfe's discovery of poetry. Fully does *Look Homeward, Angel* deserve the rather generally agreed-upon opinion that it is the most lyrical novel ever written by an American. There are many ways in which Wolfe used poetry. Besides the rhythmic lines, the colorful phrasing, the symbolic images, and the leitmotifs, Wolfe picked up from Joyce a method of using well-known phrases from classical poetry, verbatim or in paraphrase, to balance Eugene's everyday world. In this fashion was Eugene able to rout his enemies in secret and to comment upon the commonplace. For instance, noticing a streetcleaner at his vulgar labor (in that most Joycean of chapters, number 24), the boy's mind runs to Gray's line, "Let not Ambition mock their useful toil." Taunted by his friend's reasoning that it paid to be a Christian because church membership was good for business, Eugene thinks with Coleridge: "To walk together to the kirk, with a goodly company."

Such a scheme is not, of course, inherently poetic. More to the point is the chapter on Ben's funeral (number 37), where Wolfe leaves prose far behind, and even poetry merges into music. Like the last scene of *Götterdämmerung*, a whole symphony of themes is repeated and pulsed toward the transcendent triumph of life over death.

In the last chapter, the meeting of Eugene with Ben's ghost provides Wolfe with an opportunity to drift into pure fantasy; and to match the fantasy are the cadenced phrases and suggestive terms. "I shall lift no stone upon the hills," Eugene says to the ghost in nonrealistic expression; "I shall find no door in any city. But in the city of myself, upon the continent of my soul, I shall find the forgotten language, the lost world, a door where I may enter, and music strange as any ever sounded; I shall haunt you, ghost, along the labyrinthine ways until — until? O Ben, my ghost, an answer?"

Wolfe's use of poetry must take into account, too, his dithyrambic paragraphs which delight in sensuous impressions. Sound and sight passages are not unusual in prose fiction, but Wolfe is one of the few writers for whom the pleasures of smell can be prolonged for page after page. All the senses are keenly at work in his descriptions of food, in which sections even Dickens is rivaled. Here is a delectable account succinctly covering a day at the Gant household:

> In the morning they rose in a house pungent with breakfast cookery, and they sat at a smoking table loaded with brains and eggs,

ham, hot biscuit, fried applies seething in their gummed syrups,
honey, golden butter, fried steak, scalding coffee. Or there were
stacked batter-cakes, rum-colored molasses, fragrant brown sau-
sages, a bowl of wet cherries, plums, fat juicy bacon, jam. At the
mid-day meal, they ate heavily: a huge hot roast of beef, fat buttered
lima-beans, tender corn smoking on the cob, thick red slabs of sliced
tomatoes, rough savory spinach, hot yellow corn-bread, flaky biscuits, a deep-dish peach and apple cobbler spiced with cinnamon,
tender cabbage, deep glass dishes piled with preserved fruits —
cherries, pears, peaches. At night they might eat fried steak, hot
squares of grits fried in egg and butter, pork-chops, fish, young fried
chicken.

If such a passage is less than lyric poetry, it must be remembered
that Wolfe had many styles at his command. Poetry and realism
are inextricably compounded in the slice-of-life portions of the book,
especially when they concern the early morning activities of various
folk in Altamont. At such times Wolfe wrote in Joycean sentences
to his heart's content.

When in a jolly mood, Wolfe could turn to parody and, particularly when he was telling of Eugene's daydreams, mock the sentimental fiction which went for literature in Altamont. Or he could
ridicule the stupid social-column writing of the newspaper, as here:

"Members of the Younger Set were charmingly entertained last
night at a dinner dance given at Snotwood, the beautiful residence
of Mr. and Mrs. Clarence Firkins, in honor of their youngest daughter, Gladys, who made her debutt this season. Mr. and Mrs. Firkins,
accompanied by their daughter, greeted each of the arriving guests
at the threshold in a manner reviving the finest old traditions of
Southern aristocracy, while Mrs. Firkins' accomplished sister, Miss
Catherine Hipkiss, affectionately known to members of the local
younger set as Roaring Kate, supervised the checking of overcoats,
evening wraps, jockstraps and jewelry . . ."

The account continues in this vein, but the paragraph is enough
to toss to the winds the claims of those who affirm that Wolfe was
without humor.

The central and simplest theme of *Look Homeward, Angel* is the
revolt of the individual from the small town, a theme uppermost in
the minds of other writers of the 1920's — Zona Gale, Sherwood
Anderson, and Sinclair Lewis, to name a few. But unlike the works

of these authors, *Look Homeward, Angel* was written at a time when the clouds of glory had not entirely passed away, at a time before the prison house had completely closed in. The stars were right; the union of Boy and Man was as nearly perfect as could ever be expected, and from this union came a lyrical quality rare in fiction.

When the work was finished, Wolfe was sure in his mind that one did not write a book to keep it forever in his memory. One writes a book to forget it. There were other experiences and other tasks, and so he turned to them.

3. Critical Analysis: The Major Themes

Richard S. Kennedy

Wolfe's *Look Homeward, Angel* as a Novel of Development

The German term, *Bildungsroman*, which can best be translated as "novel of development" or "novel of growth" has never, to my knowledge, been adequately defined or characterized as a sub-category of the novel. We recognize in the term itself the core of its meaning. It refers to a novel which has as its subject the story of a young man or young woman who goes through the struggles of growing up and in the end reaches maturity, a point at which he has sufficent understanding of life that he can bring his career somewhat under control, free from the mistakes of the past. This kind of novel has a very strong appeal for readers because the experience is common to us all and is important to us all. The appeal is not only to young people but to everyone, for we are always, all our life long, going through the process of maturing. We are always learning from experience, we are always seeking to understand the life around us, we are always wrestling with problems that affect our destinies. I would even venture to say that the

From the *South Atlantic Quarterly,* LXIII (Spring 1964), 218-226. Reprinted by permission of the Duke University Press and Richard S. Kennedy.

reader who is tired of stories about the process of maturing is tired of life.

The theme of passing from innocence to knowing is found in many short stories which treat of a climactic episode that changes the way the central character looks at life. Katherine Mansfield's *The Garden Party*, for instance, brings Laura to the point at which she has a new insight into the complexity and strangeness of the world around her. After viewing the dead body of the young working man and offering apologies for her hat, she can declare to her brother, "Isn't life————?" and she, wordless at this point, lets us supply the many words that can fit—fascinating, bewildering, enigmatic, surprising, and so on. A novel, however, will have a whole series of these illuminating experiences. The usual sequence is to bring the hero or heroine from birth up through adolescence. But the important point is that the struggle toward understanding must be dominant and the movement must be from confusion toward control. Thus *The Red Badge of Courage*, although it begins at the point the hero is going into the army, would be properly called a novel of development because the hero is put through many tests until at last he achieves manliness and courage. Wouk's *The Caine Mutiny*, which covers about the same age span for the hero and places him in the military service, does not fall in the category of the *Bildungsroman*. The great bulk of the book is devoted to questions of authority and justice. Dickens' *Great Expectations* has a complicated mystery which winds through its plot, yet it is a good example of the novel of development. Pip goes through moral floundering from which he gradually emerges toward the end of the book. On the other hand, Dostoevsky's *Crime and Punishment*, which deals with a young man and his moral groping, cannot be called a novel of development because its focus is on a social theme and a religious theme which arise out of the misapplication of a theory that has led to murder. The first half of Dreiser's *An American Tragedy* follows the pattern of the novel of growth but the last half does not. The defining characteristic, then, of the *Bildungsroman* is a series of ordeals and learning experiences through which the hero passes as if going through initiation rites at the brink of manhood.

The thematic pattern itself is very old. For example, the maturing of Telemachus is an important part of Homer's *Odyssey*. But the pattern does not turn up often until the Romantic Movement when self-consciousness became common practice in literature. Most of the great examples of the *Bildungsroman* appear in the nineteenth and twentieth centuries: Thackeray's *Pendennis*, Meredith's *Ordeal of Richard Feverel*, Melville's *Redburn*, Maugham's *Of Human Bondage*, Lawrence's *Sons and Lovers*. The list could be very long.

Thomas Wolfe's *Look Homeward, Angel* is almost a classic example. Indeed Thomas Wolfe was very perceptive about the features of the *Bildungsroman* because it was the kind of book he could handle best. He recognized, for instance, that the novel of development was actually another form of the journey novel—with life as the journey and a certain psychological geography as the ground to be covered. In the manuscript of *Look Homeward, Angel*, he placed at the beginning of his narrative the word "Anabasis," which means in Greek "a going up."[1] He took the term from Xenophon's account of the journey "up-country" of Cyrus the Persian in pursuit of the Greeks. Wolfe recognized, too, the sense of quest in the reaching out toward maturity. When he began work on his book *Of Time and the River*, he decided that the theme would be the search for a father—it was to be a symbolic search for a figure of authority. In his last book, *The Web and the Rock*, he intended that it would be about "the innocent man discovering life."[2] He planned to put on the title page a quotation from *War and Peace*, "Prince Andrei looked up at the stars and sighed; everything was so different from what he thought it was going to be."[3]

Look Homeward, Angel contains all the experiences that the apprentice-hero usually passes through, except the religious ordeal. The story presents the struggle of young Eugene Gant to free himself from his environment and particularly to break free of a possessive mother. He passes through common childhood experiences in conflict with his brothers and sisters. He opens up his imagination through the world of books. He develops sexual curiosity. He reaches out for wider horizons under the guidance of sympathetic teachers in school. He gets his first job. He finds new intellectual freedoms and bewilderments in college. He undergoes sexual initiation. He is introduced to alcohol (the sacred brew of twentieth-century initiation rites). He faces the problem of death when his favorite brother is swept away in the influenza epidemic. He falls in love

---

[1] Harvard College Library, MS 326 F. A photostat of the first page has been reproduced in George R. Preston, Jr., *Thomas Wolfe, A Bibliography* (New York, 1943), p. 24. Wolfe had translated Xenophon's *Anabasis* in his school days at the North State Fitting School in Asheville.

[2] "Author's Note" in *The Web and the Rock* (New York, 1940).

[3] See Maxwell Perkins' account in the Introduction to *Look Homeward, Angel*, "The Scribner Library," (New York, 1957), p. xii.

and endures loss of love. He makes the break from home, and, as the book comes to a close, he reaches an interpretation of life and finds a way of life that he can follow.

But the mere presence of this subject matter (or this archetypal pattern, as one may call it) is no demonstration of the literary value of the work. A novel like *The End of Roaming* by Alexander Laing or one like *A Tree Grows in Brooklyn* by Betty Smith would have this pattern too, because any autobiographical novelist or any commercial novelist can adopt the pattern and, for his ephemeral purposes, draw upon the appeals which the pattern offers. A work must have something more if we will class it as a work of art worthy of being read more than once or worthy of being studied and of being discussed. The something more will be philosophic breadth, perhaps the kind of treatment that turns the hero into Everyman (or, one should say, Every Young Man). Or to put it another way, the something more will be the handling of the material in such a way as to create an intricate and harmonious literary complex which will enhance the significance of the book as well as provide the aesthetic pleasure of the successful work of art.

In another place, I have discussed the complexity of ideas that provide a framework for the story of Eugene Gant in *Look Homeward, Angel,* and I have also tried to show how, by means of symbol and structural arrangement, Wolfe created a full and ordered world for his hero to operate in.[4] Now I would like in this study to take just one other element of Wolfe's literary endeavor and point out how it makes its contribution to the richness of this work. I want to talk about Wolfe's style. I will begin with a reminder that the American writer has a good knack for taking lowly materials and surrounding them with an aura of the great and important. Melville takes a rough crew and an odoriferous whaling vessel and by means of style and structure creates a prose epic. Tennessee Williams takes a nymphomaniac and a thug and with symbol and technical manipulation creates a profound and moving tragedy. Wolfe takes the story of a lower-middle-class boy who lives in a Southern town and creates a novel of development that transcends its restricted lineaments. By various devices, Wolfe enlarges his scene beyond the family circle and beyond town life to make us aware that Eugene is part of a very large and complex world and that he is one of the participants in the history of man. Style is one of the means by

---

[4] Richard S. Kennedy, *The Window of Memory: The Literary Career of Thomas Wolfe* (Chapel Hill, 1962), Chapter 9, "The Design of *Look Homeward, Angel.*"

which he creates a sense of variety and abundance in the book, for Wolfe has a variety of styles that he employs.

One of the narrative styles may be described as rich, sometimes overflorid, arranged in long, loose sentences, frequently made up of elements piled in a series:

> Eugene was loose now in the limitless meadows of sensation: his sensory equipment was so complete that at the moment of perception of a single thing, the whole background of color, warmth, odor, sound, taste established itself, so that later, the breath of hot dandelion brought back the grass-warm banks of Spring, a day, a place, the rustling of young leaves[;] or a page of a book, the thin exotic smell of tangerine, the wintry bite of great apples; or, as with *Gulliver's Travels,* a bright windy day in March, the spurting moments of warmth, the drip and reek of the earth-thaw, the feel of the fire.[5]

When the diction is concrete, as it is in this example, the style is very effective, particularly for communicating an atmosphere of plenitude—of a world that has so much in it that because of abundance itself it must be very good.

At times, Wolfe's prose takes on some of the qualities of the poetry of the Imagists. There are passages which are simple, metaphorical, and rhythmical in which an impression in the mind of Eugene is carried vividly to us—as, for example, when the boy thinks of his brother:

> My Brother Ben's face, thought Eugene, is like a piece of slightly yellow ivory; his high white head is knotted fiercely by his old man's scowl; his mouth is like a knife, his smile the flicker of light across a blade. His face is like a blade, and a knife, and a flicker of light: it is delicate and fierce, and scowls beautifully forever, and when he fastens his hard white fingers and his scowling eyes upon a thing he wants to fix, he sniffs with sharp and private concentration through his long pointed nose. (p. 165)

The effect of passages like this is to create the impression that life is full of vivid little moments of illumination which can be responded to and experienced intensely.

I have called passages like these poetic because they have rhythm and highly charged language, but they are just one of Wolfe's characteristic ways of saying things. There are times, however, when

---

[5] *Look Homeward, Angel* (New York, 1929), p. 81. All other page references are to this edition and will be placed in parentheses after the quotation.

he is consciously being "poetic": that is when he writes short, set pieces (he later called them dithyrambs) that have an elevated manner and a formality of address and of arrangement in his sentences. We find these inserted in various places in the book. Here is one which Wolfe has placed at the end of a scene about Eugene's first love-affair:

> Come up into the hills, O my young love. Return! O lost, and by the wind grieved, ghost, come back again, as first I knew you in the timeless valley, where we shall feel ourselves anew, bedded on magic in the month of June. There was a place where all the sun went glistering in your hair, and from the hill we could have put a finger on a star. Where is the day that melted into one rich noise? Where is the music of your flesh, the rhyme of your teeth, the dainty languor of your legs, your small firm arms, your slender fingers, to be bitten like an apple, and the little cherry-teats of your white breasts? And where are all the tiny wires of finespun maidenhair? Quick are the months of earth, and quick the teeth that fed upon this loveliness. You who were made for music, will hear music no more: in your dark house the winds are silent. (p. 456)

When a prose lyric like this elegy is very personal to Wolfe, it is an intrusion, but one would never want to banish it. It becomes a memorable passage. It remains a beautiful excrescence on the work. Its general function then is only its presence as part of the encyclopedic profusion of the book. More often, such passages are formal apostrophes, and the effect is rather of oratory than poetry. The reader has a feeling that a public spokesman is giving voice to a communal emotion or attitude. Again there is a sense of a larger world which surrounds the hero and with which he must come to terms.

There are other passages in which the style combines both the grand and the commonplace. The effect is to elevate or to ennoble the commonplace. When old Mr. Gant returns from a trip and looks over the home town, Wolfe begins the whole section with an epic style, even employing epithet: "How looked the home-earth then to Gant the Far-Wanderer?" (p. 71). The verbal contrasts that Wolfe plays with are many: he combines the rich and the spare; he exaggerates and then follows up with understatement; he joins the majestic and the vulgar, the formal and the colloquial. The effects are varied. Sometimes he is highly comical. At other times, he makes ordinary details seem to be recurrences in the endless cycles of time. For example, here is a passage which makes use of mythological allusion and high flown language about the coming of spring—when little boys play games in the street:

> Yes, and in the month when Proserpine comes back, and Ceres' dead heart rekindles, when all the woods are a tender smoky blur, and birds no bigger than a budding leaf dart through the singing trees, and when odorous tar comes spongy in the streets, and boys roll balls of it upon their tongues, and they are lumpy with tops and agated marbles; and there is blasting thunder in the night, and the soaking millionfooted rain . . . . (p. 95)

In *Look Homeward, Angel* style is used for depth as well as for breadth. Wolfe uses the stream-of-consciousness style quite frequently in the book—usually a series of phrases and images that are supposed to represent the thought-stream of the characters. Here is an example. But I will spell out the movement of thought before quoting it. Old Mr. Gant is riding through Altamont. He thinks of some of the chamber of commerce booster slogans about the town. His thought jumps to Los Angeles and its growth. He thinks then of Mr. Bowman who lives in California and who used to be in love with Mrs. Gant. This makes him think about himself and an experience with a woman in New Orleans. This then makes him remember a time long ago in New Orleans when he was robbed in a hotel room. He thinks of prostitutes in New Orleans. He then thinks of fictional heroines in stories about New Orleans. This makes him spin out a fantasy in which he plays a heroic part.

> America's Switzerland. The Beautiful Land of the Sky. Jesus God! Old Bowman said he'll be a rich man some day. Built up all the way to Pasadena. Come on out. Too late now. Think he was in love with her. No matter. Too old. Wants her out there. No fool like —— White bellies of the fish. A spring somewhere to wash me through. Clean as a baby once more. New Orleans, the night Jim Corbett knocked out John L. Sullivan. The man who tried to rob me. My clothes and my watch. Five blocks down Canal Street in my nightgown. Two A. M. Threw them all in a heap—watch landed on top. Fight in my room. Town full of crooks and pickpockets for prizefight. Make good story. Policeman half hour later. They come out and beg you to come in. Frenchwomen. Creoles. Beautiful Creole heiress. Steamboat race. Captain, they are gaining. I will not be beaten. Out of wood. Use the bacon she said proudly. There was a terrific explosion. He got her as she sank the third time and swam to shore. (pp. 74-75)

Stream-of-consciousness passages amplify the characterizations in a book. But the general impression of the excursions through the minds of the characters in *Look Homeward, Angel* is that the hidden life of the psyche, the buried life as Wolfe calls it, is teeming with activity and that human life, such as that developing in Eugene, is a mysterious but wonderful thing.

These are some examples of the narrative styles. The presence of many different dialogue styles, of course, increases the stylistic variety, particularly because most of the characters are quite distinctive in the way they speak: W. O. Gant is full of exaggeration and rhetorical flourish; Mrs. Gant carries on in the rambling, interminable manner of free association; Ben is sharp and laconic; Luke stutters. In addition there are the currents and eddies of talk in the town—the words of clerks, servants, loafers, politicians, gatherers at the lunch counters. Much of this town talk, seemingly insignificant, is like that in Wilder's *Our Town:* it reflects the rhythms of life, comings and goings, deaths and entrances. Moreover, it is good talk, with a marked colloquial flavor. Here, for example, is Gant on the streetcar:

> "Jim Bowles died while you were gone, I reckon," said the motorman.
> "What!" howled Gant. "Merciful God!" he clucked mournfully downward. "What did he die of?" he asked.
> "Pneumonia," said the motorman. "He was dead four days after he was took down."
> "Why, he was a big healthy man in the prime of life," said Gant. "I was talking to him the day before I went away," he lied convincing himself permanently that this was true. "He looked as if he had never known a day's sickness in his life."
> "He went home one Friday night with a chill," said the motorman, "and the next Tuesday he was gone." (p. 72)

Beyond this, *Look Homeward, Angel* has a number of other evidences of Wolfe's linguistic interest such as parodies of pulp fiction stories with Eugene as the hero—like the one about Bruce-Eugene Glendenning, international vagabond, who fights off the dangerous natives, and keeps back two cartridges for himself and the beautiful Veronica Mullins; or Eugene's fantasies when he comes from the motion picture theater—Eugene Gant, the Dixie Ghost, who shoots it out with Faro Jim in the Triple Y Saloon. In this book, Wolfe plays with language in dozens of ways.

What I have been trying to establish is that by means of style Wolfe has done two important things. First, he has provided a swirl of experience around his hero and made the whole experience of life and of growing up seem exciting and valuable. Second, the linguistic variety has contributed to the complexity of the little universe in which Wolfe has placed Eugene Gant and which the boy is trying to understand. In his search for understanding, Eugene has been impelled to look to the city and its crowded streets and to the multiplicity of social experience that travel and wandering seem to offer. But at the end of the book, the ghost of his brother Ben, returned from the dead, tells Eugene that he is wrong. Eugene should look inside himself for the way to understanding. "*You* are your world," says Ben. The quality and the amplitude of that world has been partly conveyed to us by means of style.

B. R. McElderry, Jr.

The Durable Humor of
Look Homeward, Angel

When Wolfe's first novel appeared in 1929 it contrasted sharply with the drab realism and despairing naturalism so prevalent in the decade since the war. The really typical book of 1929 was Ernest Hemingway's *Farewell to Arms*, which leaves its central figure numb with grief for his dead wartime love, without a shred of faith in life, in country, or in himself. *Look Homeward, Angel* was a different book. With confident good humor it turned back to an older America, primarily to the America of 1900 to 1917. That older America, as Wolfe represented it, was far from ideal. It was provincial, it was naive, it was crude. But it was exuberantly alive, and it believed in itself. It was that belief in itself that America needed to recover in the nineteen-thirties, and the popularity of Wolfe's books in the ten years from 1929 to 1939 is a testimony to the service he rendered. His untimely death in 1938 cast a Keatsian halo around his memory, and in 1939 Wolfe was a minor literary cult.

The Keatsian halo has proved unfortunate, for it has prevented recognition of Wolfe as one of the finest humorous writers in Amer-

From the *Arizona Quarterly*, XI (Summer 1955), 123-128. Reprinted by permission of the *Arizona Quarterly* and Bruce R. McElderry, Jr.

ica since Mark Twain, perhaps even better than Twain in range and variety. *A Subtreasury of American Humor* (1941), for example, included no selection from Wolfe. There has been an over-zealous concern with the "serious" side of his work: the autobiographical nature of his fiction, the importance of editorial revision by Max Perkins, the question of whether Wolfe developed an adequate "philosophy," and the extent to which he mastered artistic form. It is time to re-read *Look Homeward, Angel*, his best novel, not so much as the agonizing search for maturity by an adolescent genius, as for the wonderful gallery of comic characters remembered and created from Wolfe's journey through the early years of this century. Eugene Gant's struggle to escape from family and environment is a thoroughly American pattern, and it gives intelligible direction to the story, but it is not the main attraction, any more than the freeing of the negro slave Jim is the main attraction of *Huckleberry Finn*. In both books it is the rich panorama and the lively episodes that enthrall.

In the comfortable old times pictured in *Look Homeward, Angel* a boy's heroes were Theodore Roosevelt, Admiral Dewey, and Woodrow Wilson. William Jennings Bryan actually appears in one scene of the novel, sonorously praising to a newspaper reporter the charms of Altamont (Asheville). Veterans of the Civil War looked back over the long years with sad pride, and the Spanish-American War was a recent event, of glorious memory. Ridpath's *History of the World* was serious reading, and for entertainment there were dozens of Alger books with alliterative titles like *Sink or Swim*, the endless adventures of the Rover Boys, and *Stover at Yale*. It was the era of the *Police Gazette*, the minstrel show, and the early silent movies. Young people of a certain age—and older ones, too—sang "I Wonder Who's Kissing Her Now," "Till the Sands of the Desert Grow Cold," and "The End of a Perfect Day." All these delights, and many more, are set down in Wolfe's novel as they really were. They are amusing, as old snapshots always are, but they are true, too, and they are worth remembering without the malice that so distorts Sinclair Lewis's description of provincial America in *Main Street*.

It is the tolerance, the lack of malice, that gives distinction to Wolfe's humor in this novel. In this he is often superior to Twain, for much of Twain's humor is overshadowed by his obvious desire to score off somebody else as more stupid than himself, or sometimes to get even with himself for being stupid. Either way the temptation to bludgeon his way is strong. Wolfe is more natural, and more varied. How easily he gets his effect as he describes the meeting of

Eliza Pentland and W. O. Gant. Eliza introduces herself as a representative of the Larkin Publishing Company:

> She spoke the words proudly, with dignified gusto. Merciful God! A book-agent! thought Gant.
> "We are offering," said Eliza, opening a huge yellow book with a fancy design of spears and flags and laurel wreaths, "a book of poems called *Gems of Verse for Hearth and Fireside* as well as *Larkin's Domestic Doctor and Book of Household Remedies,* giving directions for the cure and prevention of over five hundred diseases."
> "Well," said Gant, with a faint grin, wetting his big thumb briefly, "I ought to find one that I've got out of that."
> "Why, yes," said Eliza, nodding smartly, "as the fellow says, you can read poetry for the good of your soul and Larkin for the good of your body." (p. 11)[1]

This is humor drawn from nature, requiring nothing but selection and the restraint of accurate reporting. Another passage illustrates humorous interpretation. Gant has just called his four sons for breakfast.

> "When I was your age, I had milked four cows, done all the chores, and walked eight miles through the snow by this time."
> Indeed, when he described his early schooling he furnished a landscape that was constantly three feet deep in snow, and frozen hard. He seemed never to have attended school save under polar conditions. (p. 50)

Sometimes the humorous effect is finely dramatic, as when one of Gant's sprees makes it appear that he is actually dead. Eugene's brother Ben turns to Eliza in fright.

> "Well," she said, picking her language with deliberate choosiness, "the pitcher went to the well once too often. I knew it would happen sooner or later."
> Through a slotted eye Gant glared murderously at her. Judicially, with folded hands, she studied him. Her calm eye caught the slow movement of a stealthy inhalation.
> "You get his purse, son, and any papers he may have," she directed. "I'll call the undertaker."
> With an infuriate scream the dead awakened.
> "I thought that would bring you to," she said complacently.
> He scrambled to his feet.
> "You hell-hound!" he yelled. "You would drink my heart's blood.

---

[1] Page references are to the Modern Library edition.

You are without mercy and without pity—inhuman and bloody
monster that you are." (p. 280)

Subtler, however, is the remarkable scene in which "Queen" Elizabeth, the town madam, orders from Gant a tombstone for one of her
girls.

> "And she was such a fine girl, Mr. Gant," said Elizabeth, weeping
> softly. "She had such a bright future before her. She had more
> opportunities than I ever had, and I suppose you know"—she spoke
> modestly—"what I've done." (p. 266)

Elizabeth insists on purchasing the angel, Gant's favorite piece of
statuary, and together they select a suitable inscription for the
young prostitute's monument:

> She went away in beauty's flower,
> Before her youth was spent;
> Ere life and love had lived their hour
> God called her, and she went.

No excerpt can convey a sense of the delicate balance that prevents
this scene from falling into burlesque. Gant and Elizabeth are humorous characters in a humorous situation. Wolfe lets them have
their scene without satirical interjections.

Old man Gant is Wolfe's greatest character, and it is time to recognize him as one of the most varied comic characters in American
literature. Beside him, Twain's Beriah Sellers is a shallow and tire-
some stereotype. Gant's feud with Eliza is counterpointed by his
even greater rage at her brother, Major Will Pentland. Gant's ti-
rades, his passion for food and drink, his fear of the automobile he
absentmindedly purchased, his unblinking support of the temper-
ance movement, his pride in his children—these are but a few of the
comic materials. But Gant is not the only source of humor. Eliza
herself, literal-minded and obsessed with greed, is a wonderful foil
to her turbulent husband. When Gant returned without warning
from his long ramble in the west she "explains" his return.

> "I was saying to Steve last night, 'It wouldn't surprise me if your
> papa would come rolling in at any minute now'—I just had a feeling.
> I don't know what you'd call it," she said, her face plucked inward
> by her sudden fabrication of legend, "but it's pretty strange when
> you come to think about it. I was in Garret's the other day ordering
> some things, some vanilla extract, soda, and a pound of coffee . . . ."
> Jesus God! thought Gant. It's begun again. (p. 78)

Besides Gant and Eliza, there is young Luke Gant, energetically stuttering the townspeople into buying the *Saturday Evening Post*. There are Doc Maguire and Horse Hines (the undertaker), frequently found at Uneeda Lunch No. 3. There are Eugene's teachers: Mr. Leonard clumsily justifying the study of the classics he so unimaginatively taught; Professor Torrington, the pompous Rhodes Scholar who thought Barrie more important than Shaw; and Buck Benson, who said, "Mister Gant, you make me so damned mad I could throw you out the window," but left Eugene with a permanent love of Greek. There is a wonderful account of a Shakespeare pageant (1916):

> The pageant had opened with the Voices of Past and Present—voices a trifle out of harmony with the tenor of the event—but necessary to the commercial success of the enterprise. These voices now moved voicelessly past—four frightened sales-ladies from Schwartzberg's, clad decently in cheese-cloth and sandals, who came by bearing the banner of their concern. Or, as the doctor's more eloquent iambics had it:
>
> > Fair Commerce, sister of the arts, thou, too,
> > Shalt take thy lawful place upon our stage.
>
> They came and passed: Ginsberg's—"the glass of fashion and the mould of form"; Bradley the Grocer—"When first Pomona held her fruity horn"; The Buick Agency—"the chariots of Oxus and of Ind."
> (p. 374)

And—years before Walter Mitty—there are the skillful parodies of youthful daydreaming in which Eugene Gant sees himself as Mainwaring the young minister, declaring his love to Grace the beautiful parishioner before he goes "out west"; as Bruce Glendenning, the beachcomber who saves Veronica from a band of yelling natives; and as "The Dixie Ghost," beating Faro Jim to the draw.

Despite these shining riches, there remains what Kipling called "The Conundrum of the Workshops." The work may be clever, striking, human—but "Is it Art?" It is a hard question with respect to humor. Even admirers of Dickens are embarrassed by it. And as for *Huckleberry Finn*, Twain himself authorized the shooting of persons attempting to find a motive, moral, or plot in it. It is generally thought that without these you cannot have Art. Whether they are in fact present in *Huckleberry Finn* I shall not go into, but motive, moral, and plot are reasonably in evidence in *Look Homeward, Angel*. Eugene Gant is a sensitive boy, and his journey to adulthood has point and interest. For readers today it has more point than Huck's journey on the raft. At any rate it is a more difficult journey, for Twain took care that Huck never underwent the pangs of adolescence, in which, as Keats said, "the soul is in ferment." Whatever defects in Art there may be, *Look Homeward, Angel* has many pages as funny as any in the *Subtreasury of American Humor*. If we begin with them, and tolerantly recognize that the perfect novel has not yet been written, we may come to agree with Wolfe's mother. After she read her son's novel she said: "It's not bad at all — not bad at all."

W. P. Albrecht

The Titles of *Look Homeward, Angel: A Story of the Buried Life*

For his first novel Thomas Wolfe considered the titles *The Building of a Wall* and *Alone, Alone*. From Bath, England, July 19, 1926, he wrote to Mrs. J. M. Roberts:

> I have begun work on a book, a novel, to which I may give the title of *The Building of a Wall* . . . its unity is simply this: I am telling the story of a powerful creative element trying to work its way toward an essential isolation; a creative solitude; a secret life—its fierce struggles to wall this part of its life away from birth, first against the public and savage glare of an unbalanced, nervous brawling family group; later against school, society, all the barbarous invasions of the world. In a way, the book marks a progression toward freedom; in a way toward bondage—but this does not matter: to me one is as beautiful as the other.[1]

Later, from New York in an undated letter to Mrs. Roberts, Wolfe wrote of his first novel:

From the *Modern Language Quarterly*, XI (March 1950), 50-57. Reprinted by permission of the *Modern Language Quarterly* and W. P. Albrecht.
[1] "Writing Is My Life: Letters of Thomas Wolfe," *Atlantic Monthly*, Vol. 178, No. 6 (December, 1946), 66.

I think I shall call it *Alone, Alone,* for the idea that broods over it,
and in it, and behind it is that we are all strangers upon this earth
we walk on—that naked and alone do we come into life, and alone, a
stranger, each to each, we live upon it.[2]

Each of these titles suggests isolation as the theme of the novel;
but the first implies a voluntary and, for the "creative element" at
least, a desirable isolation, while the second implies an inescapable
and undesirable one. The final choice of *Look Homeward, Angel,* sup-
ported by its context in *Lycid*as, is appropriate to both of these
themes, with the additional implication of the search consummated.
The subtitle, *A Story of the Buried Life,* is less dramatic but, in
suggested parallels to Matthew Arnold's poem, it is perhaps an even
clearer indication of the unity of the book.

The parallels in *Lycidas* and *The Buried Life* will be more evident,
however, after an examination of the two kinds of isolation in *Look
Homeward, Angel:* the inevitable and the creative.

Man's inevitable strangeness and loneliness results not only from
his inability to know others and to be known by them but from the
feeling that he once enjoyed a refuge from isolation and doubt which,
in the prison of this life, he can almost but not quite recover. Eugene's
life in *Look Homeward, Angel* is a continual search for this refuge,
apparently the same quest that Wolfe describes in "The Story of a
Novel": "man's search to find a father . . . the image of a strength
and wisdom external to this need and superior to his hunger, to
which the belief and power of his own life could be united."[3] This
refuge, the "ghost of memory" leads one to believe, was a part of
prenatal existence;[4] but rather than a heavenly home, as in Wordsworth's *Ode: Intimations of Immortality,* this prenatal life appears
to be the endless concatenation of cause and effect preceding and
shaping the circumstances of Eugene's birth and life, extending
beyond the barren South of the Pentlands to the abundance of
Gant's Pennsylvania and still farther back beyond the seas. Thus,
Eugene's preëxistence is linked with the better time of the Gants,
with "the great barns of Pennsylvania, the ripe bending of golden
grain, the plenty, the order, the clean thrift" of Oliver's boyhood in
contrast with "this vast lost earth of rickets" and the Pentlands.[5]

---

[2] "Writing Is My Life: Munich and New York," *Atlantic Monthly,* Vol. 179,
No. 1 (January, 1947), 39.
[3] "The Story of a Novel," *Saturday Review of Literature,* XIII, No. 8 (December 21, 1935), 4.
[4] *Look Homeward, Angel* (New York: Charles Scribner's Sons, 1930), pp.
37-38. Cf. pp. 81 ff.
[5] *Ibid.,* p. 5.

But the inadequacy of the past to supply Wolfe's spiritual father is the inadequacy of Gant himself, who perhaps no more than Eliza can show Eugene "the lost lane-end into heaven, a stone, a leaf, an unfound door."[6] Gant, like Eugene, also wished to become an artist, "to wreak something dark and unspeakable in him into cold stone"; but the only "stone" he found was the clumsy angel of Carrara marble, bought for $420 and finally — and regretfully — sold as a tombstone for a prostitute. Gant "never learned to carve an angel's head."[7] For Gant the past of both Pennsylvania abundance and creative imagination was gone forever — and, with it, its promise of resolving Eugene's loneliness and doubt.

> Unweave the fabric of nights and days [Eugene demands of the stranger within him]; unwind my life back to my birth; subtract me into nakedness again, and build me back with all the sums I have not counted. Or let me look upon the living face of darkness; let me hear the terrible sentence of your voice.
>
> There was nothing but the living silence of the house; no doors were opened.[8]

If his "home" were in the past, Eugene knew that he could not go home again. For freedom, security, and certitude he had to search elsewhere.

In *Look Homeward, Angel*, therefore, are suggested the three time elements that Wolfe later mentions as inherent in the material accumulated for *Of Time and the River*.

> The first and most obvious was an element of actual present time, an element which carried the narrative forward. . . . The second time element was of past time, one which represented these same characters as acting and as being acted upon by all the accumulated impact of man's experience so that each moment of their life was conditioned not only by what they experienced in that moment, but by all that they had experienced up to that moment. In addition to these two time elements, there was a third which I conceived as being time immutable . . . a kind of eternal and unchanging universe of time against which would be projected the transience of man's life. . . .[9]

For Eugene the past is lost as something separate, but it remains partly in the life-principle, continually renewing itself in transitory

---

[6] *Ibid.*, p. [2].
[7] *Ibid.*, pp. 4, 264-68.
[8] *Ibid.*, p. 494. Cf. p. 296.
[9] "The Story of a Novel," *Saturday Review of Literature,* XIII, No. 9 (December 28, 1935), 3.

forms,[10] and — what is more important in the unity of *Look Home-ward, Angel* — in the cumulation of experience that is Eugene's essential self:

> I am, [Eugene] thought, a part of all that I have touched and that has touched me, which, having for me no existence save that which I gave it, became other than itself by being mixed with what I then was, and is now still otherwise, having fused with what I now am, which is itself a cumulation of what I have been becoming.[11]

It is in this self that Eugene finally finds the promise of a desirable or creative isolation, but in the meantime he explores a different world of imagination: he becomes Bruce-Eugene of sentimental fiction, the Dixie Ghost of the movies, Ace Gant the falcon of the skies.[12] Beyond the hills of Altamont he creates a world of "golden cities" where there is no confusion, waste, or groping, where merit is rewarded with "its true deserving";[13] he builds up in himself "a vast mythology" which is all the more attractive because he knows it to be untrue; he begins "to feel that it [is] not truth that men must live for — the creative men — but for falsehood"[14] — until in the moment of insight that closes the novel, "the golden cities sicken in his eye. . . . "[15] In Eugene's imagination Ben has returned to life, convincing Eugene that "the world" is not beyond the hills of experience but in himself. " 'Where, Ben?' " Eugene asks. " 'Where is the world?' " " 'Nowhere,' " Ben replies. " '*You* are your world.' "[16] No leaf, Eugene realizes, "hangs for [him] in the forest"; he will "lift no stone upon the hills"; he will "find no door in any city"; but "in the city of [him] self" he will find the forgotten language, the lost world, "a door where [he] may enter, and music strange as any ever sounded. . . ."[17]

This microcosmic self is, apparently, the essential self of fused experience — especially sense experience — which Eugene discovered before, apparently in his twelfth year, but had neglected for the golden cities. A pattern of experience originally disparate in time but now fused by the imagination, it is distinguished from the

---

[10] *Look Homeward, Angel,* pp. 582-83.
[11] *Ibid.,* p. 192.
[12] *Ibid.,* pp. 104-08, 203, 270-75, 533.
[13] *Ibid.,* p. 193.
[14] *Ibid.,* p. 224.
[15] *Ibid.,* p. 623.
[16] *Ibid.,* p. 624.
[17] *Ibid.,* pp. 623-25.

"ghostliness" of the time-space world by "brightness" and reality.[18]
Here is Wolfe's bright world of creation. On February 2, 1930, Wolfe
wrote to Mrs. Roberts:

> experience comes into me from all points, is digested and absorbed
> into me until it becomes a part of me, and . . . the world I create is
> *always inside me,* and never *outside* me, and . . . what reality I can
> give to what I create comes only from *within.* . . . I shaped and
> created its reality from within: my *own* world, my *own* figures, my
> *own* events shaped themselves into my *own* fable there on the page
> before me, and . . . I spent no time in thinking of actual Smiths,
> Joneses, or Browns; nor do I see yet how such a thing is possible.
> If anyone thinks it is, let him take notes at street corners, and see if
> the result is a book.[19]

Furthermore, in "The Story of a Novel" Wolfe explicitly names the
"door" of his search as the door to creative power,[20] and again he
represents his creative power as issuing from his cumulative self. In
Paris in the summer of 1930, while Wolfe was working on *Of Time
and the River,* "the million forms and substances" of his life in
America swarmed in "blazing pageantry" across his mind, issuing
even from the "farthest adyt of his childhood before conscious memory had begun," yet transformed with the new wonder of discovery;
and as he resolved to find words that would bring these forms to
life in a "final coherent union," "the line and purpose of [his] life
was shaped."[21] His experiences in France in 1930, like Eugene's final
interview with Ben in *Look Homeward, Angel,* made Wolfe aware
of his source of strength as an artist. This discovery must be distinguished, of course, from merely going "home" to the past. In this
sense, it has been pointed out, Wolfe "did not go home again, finally.
He returned instead to the actual America. . . . He returned to his
senses: the exceptionally alert, acute senses that were the spring of
his art."[22] But he did not simply record sense impressions. He was
aware that his remembered experiences, modified by each other and
by new experiences, were continually fusing into a new unity.

This source of strength bears a close resemblance to the "genuine
self" of *The Buried Life.* This self is the complex of sympathy, understanding, security, freedom, and articulateness ordinarily obscured

---

[18] *Ibid.,* pp. 191-92.
[19] "Writing Is My Life: The Novelist under Fire," *Atlantic Monthly,* Vol. 179,
No. 2 (February, 1947), 55-56.
[20] "The Story of a Novel," *Saturday Review of Literature,* XIII, No. 8 (December 21, 1935), 15.
[21] *Ibid.,* XIII, 3, 15.
[22] Herbert J. Muller, *Thomas Wolfe* (Norfolk, Connecticut, 1947), p. 75.

by timid imitation and selfish competition, and but infrequently realized in moments of love. The aspect of the buried life that led Wolfe to use Arnold's phrase in the closing chapters of *Of Time and the River* is its suggestion of common humanity, for in the little French towns Eugene has rediscovered "the buried life, the fundamental structure of the great family of earth to which all men belong": a discovery that "filled him with a quiet certitude and joy."[23] This theme of common humanity is, of course, developed further in *You Can't Go Home Again*, but although it is suggested in *Look Homeward, Angel*, in his first novel Wolfe is more interested in other aspects of the buried life: its concealment and its creative power.

In *The Buried Life*, as in *Look Homeward, Angel*, "disguises" render men "alien to the rest / Of men, and alien to themselves. . . ." Furthermore, both Eugene and the "we" of Arnold's poem are searching for truth and articulateness, but the source of knowledge and power, although within Eugene and "us," is difficult to make use of. Frequently, Arnold points out, we long to discover in "our buried life" the direction of our lives — "to know / Whence our lives come and where they go." But truth and knowledge remain elusive when we assume other selves — like Bruce-Eugene of the golden cities — which, supplying only a "stupefying," "benumbing" power, do not let us "say or do" the truth. Meanwhile, just as Eugene sickened in his search for the golden cities, we are made "melancholy" by "airs" and "floating echoes" from the "soul's subterranean depth unborne / As from an infinitely distant land. . . ." But in rare moments of insight, achieved through love, come articulateness, knowledge, and direction.

> The eye sinks inward, and the heart lies plain,
> And what we mean, we say, and what we would, we know.
> A man becomes aware of his life's flow. . . .
> The hills where his life rose,
> And the sea where it goes.

In *Look Homeward, Angel*, as well, strong feeling for a loved one precedes moments of insight and the resulting awareness of direction in life. After the death of Ben, closest of all the Gants to Eugene, Eugene first fully realizes the irrevocableness of the past and the continuity of the life-principle, eternal and unchanging, behind the progression of evanescent forms.[24] The last chapter, in which the answer to Eugene's search is made most explicit, follows a moment

---

[23] *Of Time and the River* (New York: Charles Scribner's Sons, 1946), p. 755.
[24] *Look Homeward, Angel*, pp. 582-83.

of inarticulate feeling between Eugene and Eliza.[25] And, of course, it is Ben once more through whom the final revelation of self is made to Eugene. In this moment of vision, the direction of Eugene's life becomes plain: his path lies always ahead, never back toward the irrecoverable past, but into the future of the essential, creative self, which can never be the same as it has been. He was "like a man who stands upon a hill above the town he has left, yet does not say 'the town is near,' but turns his eyes upon the distant soaring ranges."[26]

These parallels, of course, are not drawn to suggest that *Look Homeward, Angel* is merely a dramatization of *The Buried Life* or that Wolfe borrowed a system of thought from Arnold. The essential self as a spiritual being obscured by imitation and conformity in earthly life, as the one, real, enduring self beyond or above the many, apparent, and passing selves, and as the source of truth and creative power realized in moments of emotion, is a familiar concept in Neo-Platonic and transcendental thought. To mention only a few writers who left other traces in Wolfe's novels, it is a central concept in Wordsworth, Coleridge, Shelley, Emerson, and Whitman.

In Wordsworth's *Ode: Intimations of Immortality* the emotional cycle of incarnation—the memory of a bright existence before birth, the sense of loss in the dark prison of worldly life, the obscuring shadow of imitation, and the brightening promise of recovery — is much the same as Eugene's. Wolfe's resolution of the lost-home theme, like Wordsworth's, is partly in the "soothing thoughts" from "human suffering" and partly in foreseeing, after death, reintegration with the eternal forces animating the phenomenal world; but Wolfe, like Emerson in "Self-Reliance," stresses the realization of self, and its concomitant powers, in this life.[27]

---

[25] *Ibid.*, p. 615.

[26] *Ibid.*, pp. 625-26.

[27] Cf., for suggested parallels to the *Ode,* Maxwell Geismar, *Writers in Crisis* (Boston, 1942), p. 194 [See page 56 of this collection.]; and Monroe M. Stearns, "The Metaphysics of Thomas Wolfe," *College English,* VI (January, 1945), 195-99. Mr. Stearns shows Wolfe's early and continued interest in Wordsworth and his recognition, in the poetry of both Wordsworth and Coleridge, of his own feeling toward life. Book III of *The Prelude,* Mr. Stearns continues, suggested Wolfe's refrain "a stone, a leaf, an unfound door," which expresses (1) the loss of the protector-mother relationship and (2) the search for a father, which "becomes, as well, the search for God." The "door," therefore, is "the entrance both back to the protective maternal womb and to the heaven from which, in the Platonic doctrine, we in our essence come." This interpretation of Wolfe's lost-home metaphor is helpful and, in these terms, unexceptionable; but it remains, perhaps, misleadingly metaphorical. "God" suggests freedom, security, and certitude; but it also suggests, as in the *Ode,* a sentient Being immanent in man, at once his origin and his destiny; whereas Wolfe, in resolving the lost-home theme, emphasizes, more than these aspects of God, the discovery of his (or Eugene's) source of strength as an artist.

Eugene's imaginative process also recalls Coleridge's distinction betweeen imagination and fancy. In fact, in describing Eugene's power of imagination Wolfe uses Coleridge's own word "esemplastic."[28] Coleridge classifies imagination as primary and secondary. The former is "the living power and prime agent of all human perception, and . . . a repetition in the finite mind of the eternal act of creation in the infinite I AM." For Eugene, too, perception and creation are one and the same; all that he touched and that touched him had "no existence save that which [he] gave it. . . ." In the sense that the primary imagination *creates*, the secondary imagination may be said to *re-create*; "co-existing with the conscious will," it is the translating of creative power into a work of art. Whereas fancy deals with "fixities and definites," secondary imagination "dissolves, diffuses, dissipates, in order to re-create: or . . . at all events, it struggles to idealize and to unify."[29] Similarly, Wolfe strove to transmute the fused experience of his cumulative self into a unity of verbal expression, repudiating — with the "notes at street corners" — the "fixities and definites" of fancy.

Thus, the form and ideas suggested by "the buried life" could be accounted for by influences other than Arnold's; but because Wolfe's thought and imagery had formed a pattern resembling Arnold's in *The Buried Life,* Wolfe found in this poem an accurate and suggestive subtitle for his novel.

In view of Eugene's question and Ben's answer, "Look Homeward" appears to be Ben's admonition to Eugene to find refuge within himself. "Home" also suggests Eugene's home in Altamont (and Wolfe's in Asheville), the prenatal complex of cause and effect, and perhaps the inextinguishable life-principle reflected in the passing forms of life. But the essential self of Eugene's accumulated experience comprises all three of these "homes" transmuted into material for artistic creation. Self-reliance at least promises to open the door to creative solitude.

There remains to be examined Wolfe's use of the word "angel." In *Lycidas* the "Angel" is evidently that "of the guarded Mount," who is asked to look nearer home rather than off to "Namancos and Bayona's hold" and to have pity on the drifting corpse of Lycidas. By analogy to this situation, Ben would seem to be the angel and Eugene Lycidas. "Angel" suggests a spirit secure in eternal life;

---

[28] Spelled "esymplastic" in *Look Homeward, Angel,* p. 201.
[29] *Biographia Literaria,* Everyman's Library (London, 1934), Chap. XIII, pp. 159-60.

"ghost" a spirit lost in death. The opposition of these terms occurs first at the beginning of the novel, where the passage prefacing Chapter One ends with the line "O lost, and by the wind grieved, ghost come back again," and where, as though in response to this cry, the next page begins with the title "Look Homeward, Angel!" Again, in the last chapter Ben repeats that he is "not dead," that he is "not a ghost," so that Eugene wonders whether he himself is not the ghost.[30] Ben is not explicitly named "angel," it is true, but the identification is further implied by the stone angels' coming to life when Ben returns and, when he departs, by their freezing again into immobility.[31]

Among the more frequent allusions to the title are Ben's bitter asides to his "dark Angel"; whereas Eugene finds an angel or guardian in Ben himself. This is a dark angel, too — dark even when Ben returns from the dead, his face obscured by the "shadow of his gray felt hat. . . ."[32] But as his interview with Eugene continues, Ben becomes "bright"; for he is alive not only in the universal life-principle — in "flower and leaf," in the "majestic processionals" of the seasons[33] — but also in Eugene's cumulative self. This "death-less" and "unchanging Ben," like other experiences integral with Eugene's true self, is the timeless cumulation of all the Bens that Eugene knew, the "one" compounded of "many." "Eugene watched the army of himself and Ben, which were not ghosts. . . ." No longer dark, "the fierce bright horde of Ben spun in and out of its deathless loom."[34] Also in this second aspect of his aliveness, Ben is again linked with the stone angels in the shop. A stone angel in a Baltimore street first incited Gant to carve in stone;[35] the angels in his shop stand for his creative impulse and, in their marble deadness, for its frustration. But with Ben's return the angels come alive and with them the creative power within Eugene. As the angels melt from their stone rigidity, so does the angel Ben "melt with ruth," and the "hapless" Eugene is wafted "homeward." From "the shores and sounding seas" where his "bones are hurled" Lycidas is "mounted high" in heaven. He is recalled from death to life, from the darkness of the sinking day-star to its brilliance in the morning sky, from being lost to being found, from imprisonment and impotence to

[30] *Look Homeward, Angel,* pp. 618-20.
[31] *Ibid.,* pp. 618, 620, 626.
[32] *Ibid.,* p. 617.
[33] *Ibid.,* pp. 582-83, 623.
[34] *Look Homeward, Angel,* p. 622.
[35] *Ibid.,* p. 4.

freedom and power. Although limited to life in this world, this is the metamorphosis sought for, and partly consummated, by Eugene in *Look Homeward, Angel*. In this sense, Lycidas-Eugene is at least on his way to becoming an "angel," and the title is appropriately addressed to Eugene as well as to Ben.

Therefore, the themes of both inevitable and creative isolation and the resolution of the former into the latter are implicit in the titles finally chosen for *Look Homeward, Angel*. "A Story of the Buried Life" refers to the essential self, which in Arnold's poem has the same qualities as in *Look Homeward, Angel*: especially strangeness and latent power; whereas "Look Homeward, Angel" suggests the transition, and the method of transition, from mere lostness in isolation toward an integrated, creative solitude.

Larry Rubin

Thomas Wolfe and the Lost Paradise

Although Maxwell Geismar has pointed out that the main theme of *Look Homeward, Angel* is "the lost paradise,"[1] the fact that this motif can be viewed as the basic organizing theme of Thomas Wolfe's entire tetralogy has gone largely unrecognized. The over-all theme of Wolfe's four major novels has been variously described as "growth," "a pilgrimage," "a pilgrim's progress," and "an odyssey."[2]

From *Modern Fiction Studies,* XI (Autumn 1965), 250-258. Copyright © 1965 by the Purdue Research Foundation. Reprinted by permission of the Purdue Research Foundation and Larry Rubin.
[1] Maxwell Geismar, "The Diary of a Provincial," in Richard Walser, ed., *The Enigma of Thomas Wolfe: Biographical and Critical Selections* (Cambridge, Massachusetts: Harvard University Press, 1953), p. 110–hereafter cited as *Enigma.* Geismar points out that the theme of the lost paradise is fairly common in European literature down to Wordsworth, but says that Wolfe may be unique among modern writers in this respect. [See page 57 of this collection. —— EDITOR.]
[2] See, for example, Herbert J. Muller, *Thomas Wolfe* (Norfolk, Connecticut: New Directions Books, 1947), pp. 67, 74, 153-154; Nathan L. Rothman, "Thomas Wolfe and James Joyce: A Study in Literary Influence," *Enigma,* p. 266. Monroe M. Stearns, "The Metaphysics of Thomas Wolfe," *Enigma,* p. 199; and Joseph Warren Beach, *American Fiction: 1920-1940* (New York: The Macmillan Company, 1941), p. 179. At two places in his book, however, Muller names other themes as the central one; at one place it is "lost America" (p. 121); at another it is "the transient life of man on this earth" (p. 187). W. M. Frohock says the main theme is that of "being lost in America" ("Of Time and Neurosis," *Enigma,* p. 233).

Franz Schoenberner's comment is more or less typical: he sees the tetralogy as a "pilgrim's progress from the exalted, rhapsodic lyricism, the youthful turmoil and ecstasy of his first book to the manly composure, the profound ethical awareness of his 'Credo' in the last chapter of *You Can't Go Home Again*."[3]

The primary reason the critics have failed to perceive the essential role played by the theme of the lost paradise is that the relation between this concept and the other leading themes of the novels has never been adequately described. Although the idea of the lost paradise comes to the surface but infrequently after *Look Homeward, Angel,* most of the themes that seem to dominate *Of Time and the River, The Web and the Rock,* and *You Can't Go Home Again* owe their existence, both logically and aesthetically, to this great parent theme. In this paper I shall first discuss the theme as idea and then outline its relation to Thomas Wolfe's other recurrent concepts. The main part of the paper, however, will be given over to tracing this idea through the tetralogy by analyzing and tracing the various recurrent images that embody and convey it. By using this approach, I hope to make clear the way in which the theme and its associated images provide a connecting strand which links scattered parts of the novels.

The nature of this theme is partially clarified by Thomas Lyle Collins, who quotes the prefatory poem to the novel, with its expression of a vague yearning for "a stone, a leaf, an unfound door." "From this," he says, "we may extract a brutally prosaic statement of Wolfe's theme: all through life we are searching for some sign—'a stone, a leaf, a door'—which will open up to us the universe of perfection and enchantment which we feel vaguely to have left behind us when we were born. The implication is that our souls have been torn from this enchanted heaven and imprisoned in corporeal frames here on earth."[4] Specifically linking this concept with Wordsworth's idea of pre-existence in the "Ode on Intimations of Immortality from Recollections of Early Childhood," Monroe M. Stearns sees the stone-leaf-door phrase as Wolfe's means of expressing "the psychological pangs of birth." "The loss of relationship with his protector-mother," Stearns continues, "is symbolized for Wolfe in Wordsworth's nostalgia for that spiritual home whence comes the

[3] Franz Schoenberner, "My Discovery of Thomas Wolfe," *Enigma,* p. 292.
[4] Thomas Lyle Collins, "Wolfe's Genius vs. His Critics," *Enigma,* pp. 170-171. Collins also notes the obvious Wordsworthian overtones of this idea.

soul trailing its clouds of glory. Life thus became to Wolfe a penance for the sin of having been born and having left that apocalyptic world of Plato, Plotinus, Wordsworth, and Coleridge, in which the soul knows its true nature and is free."[5] The fullest discussion of this theme, however, is that by Louis D. Rubin, Jr., who states: "The evidence is strong that though Thomas Wolfe may have felt the logical necessity to disavow a belief [in] pre-existence and the supernatural, his instinctive mysticism took artistic precedence over the logic."[6] Rubin sees this theme in the Webber cycle as well as the Gant cycle,[7] and as I shall show, it can actually be traced throughout the tetralogy.

True, the theme of the lost paradise appears much less frequently in the last three books than it does in the first, but what makes this concept so important even after *Look Homeward, Angel* is the fact that most of the themes that *do* seem paramount spring directly or indirectly from this one. Take, for example, the author's obsession with time and his attempts to recapture the past through memory. Since the novelist feels that birth has brought loss of enchantment, and since his birth was an event taking place at a point in the past, any means by which he can make the past live again will serve to bring him closer to the Elysium he once knew. Events prior to his birth are preferable, since then he was still in paradise; but events of his own childhood are also eminently worthy of re-creation, because the echoes of the lost paradise were then still relatively strong and because during his childhood he still enjoyed a measure of the security and innocence his soul had known in heaven.

Then, too, there is the theme of alienation. Because he has lost his pre-natal paradise, the hero feels like a stranger on the earth; he suffers a profound and haunting feeling of "not belonging"—a feeling he never overcomes until, near the end of his story, his maturing sense of social consciousness makes him aware that he is indeed a member of the family of humankind. Finally, we find that the great theme of the quest for an earthly paradise of love and fame is motivated by the hero's sense of having lost his heavenly one and by his resulting desire to find a substitute paradise in *this* life as a kind of

---

[5] *Enigma,* p. 202, Stearns traces the stone-leaf-door phrase to Wordsworth's *Prelude.* See also Louis D. Rubin, Jr., *Thomas Wolfe: The Weather of His Youth* (Baton Rouge: University of Louisiana Press, 1955), p. 61. Collins, however, suggests that the source of these symbols may be Archibald MacLeish's poem, "Ars Poetica" (*Enigma,* pp. 165-166).
[6] Louis D. Rubin, Jr., p. 67. See also W. P. Albrecht, "Time as Unity in Thomas Wolfe," *Enigma,* pp. 241-242, and Stearns, *Enigma,* p. 204.
[7] Louis D. Rubin, Jr., pp. 62-63.

compensation. These, then, are the major themes whose parallel development provides the contrapuntal design of Wolfe's novels; but it is well to note here that it is this central and generative theme of the lost paradise which supplies the motivating power, so to speak, for each of the others. Thus one element in Wolfe's thematic design is the fact that his prominent themes spring from a single source. Indeed, one might almost say they start from a single point, for a number of the author's recurrent themes and images have their genesis in the brief prose poem which prefaces *Look Homeward, Angel:*

> . . . a stone, a leaf, an unfound door; of a stone, a leaf, a door. And of all the forgotten faces.
> Naked and alone we came into exile. In her dark womb we did not know our mother's face; from the prison of her flesh have we come into the unspeakable and incommunicable prison of this earth.
> Which of us has known his brother? Which of us has looked into his father's heart? Which of us has not remained forever prison-pent? Which of us is not forever a stranger and alone?
> O waste of loss, in the hot mazes, lost, among bright stars on this most weary unbright cinder, lost! Remembering speechlessly we seek the great forgotten language, the lost lane-end into heaven, a stone, a leaf, an unfound door. Where? When?
> O lost, and by the wind grieved, ghost, come back again. (*LH*, p. 2)[8]

Besides the theme of the lost paradise, expressed here by the stone-leaf-door image, we find in this passage images relating to the themes of alienation, the quest, and the wish to halt the flow of time. Thus, at the outset of the tetralogy, Wolfe presents the initial statement of the major motifs he will later develop in contrapuntal fashion. Of these, the theme of the lost paradise is dominant.

Let us then trace this theme through Wolfe's novels in terms of its recurrent images. Clearly, the major image which gives substance to this concept is the stone-leaf-door set of symbols. As Stearns puts it, this refrain "symbolizes not only the pain of birth but also those tokens (like Wordsworth's rainbow, rose, tree, and pansy) which remind the mortal of his immortal nature."[9] It is not unlikely that the

---

[8] Wolfe's four major novels—*Look Homeward, Angel, Of Time and the River, The Web and the Rock,* and *You Can't Go Home Again*—are cited in this paper as *LH, TR, WR,* and *YC,* respectively.
[9] *Enigma,* p. 204. But cf. E. K. Brown, "Thomas Wolfe: Realist and Symbolist," *Enigma,* pp. 219-220.

stone and the leaf appealed to Wolfe as familiar natural objects by means of which one can conjure up the great world of the out-of-doors. A Wordsworthian love of nature is characteristic of Wolfe's young hero, Eugene, who lives in the Southern Appalachians; and the awesome beauty of the mountain region, as it impressed itself upon the receptive consciousness of the child, probably comes closest to inspiring the feelings of sublimity and freedom associated with the lost land of pre-existence. The door, on the other hand, is a man-made object. Its presence here foreshadows its use as an important image of the quest for an earthly paradise of love and fame in the city—a quest on which the hero prepares to embark at the end of *Look Homeward, Angel*. It is significant that near the end of this book, when Eugene tells himself that he has indeed lost the paradise of pre-existence, he does so in terms that clearly link the stone and the leaf with a rural, sylvan setting—the environment he knew as a child—and the door with an urban setting—the environment he is to know as a young man: " 'And no leaf hangs for me in the forest; I shall lift no stone upon the hills; I shall find no door in any city' " (*LH*, p. 625).

In tracing this image through the tetralogy after its initial appearance in the prefatory poem to *Look Homeward, Angel*, we find that it recurs a number of times in that book but is virtually abandoned in the later books, as the hero leaves his mountain home to find a door to some earthly paradise.[10] It is in Eugene's moods of loneliness, melancholy, or fantasy that the refrain is wont to recur in the first novel. Thus on his paper route at half-past three in the morning, he hears strange, ghostly voices calling to him in the darkness: "Here, Eugene. The way is here, Eugene. Have you forgotten? The leaf, the rock, the wall of light. Lift up the rock, Eugene, the leaf, the stone, the unfound door. Return, return" (*LH*, pp. 295-296). Similarly, indulging in his romantic fantasies, Eugene, we learn, "wanted opulent solitude. His dark vision burned on kingdoms under the sea, on windy castle crags, and on the deep elf kingdoms at the earth's core. He groped for the doorless land of faery, that illimitable haunted country that opened somewhere below a leaf or a stone" (*LH*, pp. 276-277).[11]

Several of the stone-leaf-door references are related to the death of Ben, Eugene's older brother, the one person he ever seems to feel

---

[10] The stone-leaf-door image appears in *TR*, p. 160; another passage alludes to the stone and leaf only (*TR*, p. 29). There is no significant reference to the image in the Webber cycle.

[11] Ben too seeks a stone, a leaf, a door (*LH*, p. 113).

really close to. Through death, perhaps, Ben has regained the lost paradise; for Eugene and his brother Luke speak of the dead Ben "as of one who had defeated pain, and had joyously escaped" (*LH*, p. 563).[12] Besides, he was merely a visitor on earth: "Like Apollo, who did his penance to the high god in the sad house of King Admetus, he came, a god with broken feet, into the gray hovel of this world. And he lived here a stranger, trying to recapture the music of the lost world, trying to recall the great forgotten language, the lost faces, the stone, the leaf, the door" (*LH*, p. 557). Alone at Ben's grave at night, Eugene begins a kind of chant, part of which is as follows: "The star over the town, the light over the hill, the sod over Ben, night over all. . . . Over us all is something. Star, night, earth, light . . . light . . . O lost . . . a stone . . . a leaf . . . a door . . ." (*LH*, p. 582).[13] And at the end of the book, when Eugene sees Ben's ghost on the town Square, he tells the shade:

> "There is something I have lost and have forgotten. I can't remember, Ben."
> "What do you want to remember?" said Ben.
> "A stone, a leaf, an unfound door. And the forgotten faces." (*LH*, p. 621)

This constant conjunction of Ben and the dominant symbol of the lost paradise puts him, like Eugene, in the category of those who perceive the loss of their prenatal heaven and so adds to the impact of this theme by uniting it with the hero's closest companion. Just as the theme of filial ingratitude in *King Lear* is emphasized and strengthened by its appearance in the Gloucester subplot as well as in the main plot, so Wolfe's theme of the lost paradise is reinforced by its association with Ben as well as with Eugene.

The other recurrent images of the lost paradise are mainly echoes of sounds half-heard—much like Shelley's mystical "memory of music fled" ("Hymn to Intellectual Beauty," 1. 10). Dominating this group are the sounds of a bell and a horn. When Eugene is still in his crib, for example, "somewhere within or without his consciousness he heard a great bell ringing faintly, as if it sounded undersea, and as he listened, the ghost of memory walked through his mind, and for a moment he felt that he had almost recovered what he had lost" (*LH*, p. 38).[14] Similarly, when he leaves the

---

[12] See also *LH*, p. 560.
[13] All ellipses in this passage, except the first, are Wolfe's.
[14] Louis D. Rubin, Jr., also cites this passage, implying that the undersea bell is a reminder of Wordsworthian, Platonic pre-existence (p. 62).

college campus at Pulpit Hill after graduation, "he heard, as from the sea-depth of a dream, far-faint, the mellow booming of the campus bell" (*LH*, p. 604). Here the actual ringing of an ordinary campus bell is adapted by Wolfe through the magic of connotative diction ("sea-depth of a dream, far faint") to the purpose of evoking the concept of the lost paradise. Another sound half-heard is that of a horn. "Far-forested, a horn-note wound" (*LH*, p. 296), Wolfe writes. When Ben dies, Eugene compares the crow of the midnight cock to "a far horn sounding under sea . . . a warning to all the men who are about to die, and to the ghosts that must go home" (*LH*, pp. 560-561). It should be noted that all these sounds of bell and horn are musical in tone; moreover, in their transmission through the thick, reluctant mediums of forest or sea, they become largely muffled or muted. Thus they are remote and far-off, and so they may be considered appropriate echoes of a lost paradise. Besides, since it is the soul, not the body, which dwells in paradise before birth, such sounds as those Eugene hears are apprehended, not by the physical ear, but by the soul. Hence, in all these references to ghostly echoes, sound and mystical connotation conspire to produce the undeniable impact upon the reader.

But this eerie music is not limited simply to that made by horns and bells; for music—*qua* music—faintly heard, or even "unheard," is another of the reminders of the lost paradise which occasionally haunt Eugene. Alone in Norfolk, for example, the adolescent hero thinks of his family "as if they were ghosts. The world itself turned ghost. . . . Everything was old. Everything was dying. A vast aerial music, forever far-faint, like the language of his forgotten world, sounded in his ears" (*LH*, p. 521). The image of music sometimes appears in combination with that of the horn note. In his vision on the Square at the end of *Look Homeward, Angel,* for instance, Eugene sees himself walking his old newspaper route in the silent predawn hours, "drugged in the magic of unheard music, listening for the far-forested horn-note" (*LH*, p. 622). Also in this vision, Wolfe declares that Eugene "heard inland murmurs of lost seas, the far interior music of the horns" (*LH*, p. 625). All these images of music, horn and bell included, thus take their place beside the stone-leaf-door refrain as concrete embodiments of the recurrent theme of the lost paradise—the first and most basic of the several motifs in Wolfe's contrapuntal design.

After the first book, however, the number of images having direct reference to the Wordsworthian lost paradise drops sharply, because now the hero takes up his quest for an earthly substitute—a quest which is a consequence of his loss of the original, prenatal paradise and which has its own set of images. Aside from several allusions in *Of Time and the River* to the stone-leaf-door image,[15] there are a few references to muted sounds, the tugging of a leaf upon a tree limb, and other distant or ephemeral phenomena. The "sound" of spring in New England, for example, is "the sound of something lost and elfin and half-dreamed, half-heard" (*TR*, p. 139). Also, as a man, George Webber, the hero of the second half of the tetralogy, remembers his childhood ecstasy at seeing "the passing of a cloud upon the massed green of a hill," "the faint and broken ringing of a bell in afternoon," "the tugging of a leaf upon a bough" (*WR*, pp. 606-607). Moreover, the idea of "hearing" physically nonexistent music helps explain one of the several prefatory mottoes to *Of Time and the River*—a quotation, ascribed to Socrates, from the Platonic dialogue "Crito": " 'Crito, my dear friend Crito, that, believe me, that is what I seem to hear, as the Corybants hear flutes in the air, and the sound of those words rings and echoes in my ears and I can listen to nothing else.' " The words Socrates hears are those of the Athenian laws, admonishing him to obey them; but the image of the flute is an appropriate addition to Wolfe's cluster of images involving ghostly music. Besides, Wolfe, like Socrates, could be compared to the Corybants in that his soul too is ravished by the ghostly tones of harmony that he hears. Once more, the common denominator of all such images of the lost paradise is the fact that they are essentially *echoes*—insubstantial tokens of a spiritually felt, intuitively apprehended reality. As Wolfe himself says, ". . . if a man should dream of heaven, and, waking, find within his hand a flower as token that he had really been there—what then, what then?" (*LH*, p. 436).

Wolfe's lingering sense of the enchanted period of pre-existence also helps account for his intense feeling for the wonder and mystery of life, as he bathes in the afterglow of paradise. As Muller remarks, Wolfe has a "quick feeling" for "the enchantments of routine modern experience."[16] This feeling finds expression in the aura of magic which the author attempts to cast over the scenes and objects encountered or visualized by his hero. A great deal of what Eugene-George sees or thinks about is "magic," "elfin," "enchanted," "haunted," or otherwise linked to the realm of "faery." Nor are these

---

[15] See note 10, above.
[16] Muller, p. 72. See also Pamela Hansford Johnson, *Hungry Gulliver: An English Critical Appraisal of Thomas Wolfe* (New York: Charles Scribner's Sons, 1948), pp. 20-21.

images of magic limited to *Look Homeward, Angel;* rather, they recur constantly throughout the four novels, thus helping link the multi-farious episodes which crowd the tetralogy. Boston, for example, is a "magic city" (*TR*, p. 160); similarly, New York City has "magical and shining air" and "enchanted weather" (*TR*, p. 417). In *The Web and the Rock* Wolfe refers to "the green-gold drowsy magic of our meditations" (*WR*, p. 26). The last book in the tetralogy alludes to "the magic dark of summer" (*YC*, p. 40) and refers to Germany as "the Land of the Enchanted Forest, land of legends and the magic of the elves" (*YC*, p. 496).

The haunting stillness of a moonlight setting is particularly likely to evoke images of magic in Wolfe's work. Tracing this indirect suggestion of the lost paradise through the tetralogy, we find a number of illustrations. One night when Eugene is alone with his childhood sweetheart, Laura James, for example, Wolfe writes, "The moonlight fell upon the earth like a magic unearthly dawn. It wiped away all rawness, it hid all sores. It gave all common and familiar things . . . a uniform bloom of wonder. . . . The moonlight fell upon them, bathing their flesh in a green pallor, and steeping them in its silence. . . . They gazed at each other in that elfin light . . ." (*LH*, p. 442). When he visits his friend Joel Pierce at the latter's estate on the Hudson, Eugene thinks the house looks enchanted in the moonlight—like a "dream house," a "magic house" (*TR*, p. 515). And the author asserts that "in the white light of the moon the spires and ramparts of Manhattan were glittering with cold magic" (*YC*, p. 315).

All these references to magic constitute a mere handful of examples, for the complete list of images relating to magic is seemingly endless.[17] Yet even these few illustrations are enough to indicate the broad range of subject matter treated as magical and thus provided with a coherent strand of meaning. Although, as we have seen, in the books after *Look Homeward, Angel* the theme of the lost paradise is no longer dominant, it is not entirely absent; for these recurrent images of magic in the later books echo the theme; and their continual reappearance indicates that, though this concept may be overshadowed by the new theme of the quest, it is never completely submerged. Indeed, the idea of the lost paradise cannot be submerged, since it gives rise to the quest-motif, as well as to other themes, and thereby remains the central and controlling concept in Wolfe's thematic pattern.

---

[17] *TR* and *WR* contain the bulk of such references to magic, but there is a goodly scattering of images of magic in the other two novels.

In all these varied images involving direct and indirect references to prenatal glory, then, one perceives an eerie awareness of the mysterious beauty of life—a haunting sense of something enchanted which the hero may have known more purely, or seen more clearly, in some previous existence. A bell, a horn—muted, half-heard; a stone, a leaf, a door; aerial music far-faint; the magic that invests all things he sees or envisions; the weird ghostliness of "moon-drunk" settings—all these images become appropriate means, in this romantic context, of embodying and conveying the dimly seen glimpses, the barely heard echoes, of Wolfe's lost paradise. Finally, by linking so many scenes and events upon the thread of this one central, recurrent, and generative theme, these recurrent images impose a kind of unity upon the huge variety of incidents and episodes found in the novels.

J. Russell Reaver and Robert I. Strozier

From "Thomas Wolfe and Death"

Students of Thomas Wolfe's fiction fully realize its autobiographical basis, but his former critics have overlooked the intimate connection between his protagonists' evolving attitudes toward death and the corresponding maturity of Wolfe. The effusive Eugene Gant of *Look Homeward, Angel* forms a striking contrast to the more restrained George Webber of *The Web and the Rock* and *You Can't Go Home Again*. A major aspect of this difference in Wolfe's heroes lies in the significance they place on death. This study traces Wolfe's achievement of emotional maturity and shows the corresponding effect that his development had on his stylistic methods.

Wolfe's first novel *Look Homeward, Angel: A Story of the Buried Life* derives its title from Milton's "Lycidas," a poem of isolation and the growth of self-awareness. The title is noteworthy because it combines the two central kinds of isolation that troubled Wolfe throughout his life: the inevitable separation of physical death and

From the *Georgia Review,* XVI (Fall 1962), 330-337, 350. Reprinted by permission of the *Georgia Review* and J. Russell Reaver and Robert I. Strozier.

the agonizing isolation of creative defeat.[1] Wolfe thought of isolation as a kind of death, yet it held a tantalizing promise.

In *Look Homeward, Angel* Eugene Gant's existence becomes an emotional combat against death and the pressures denying him psychological freedom. Eugene's unceasing struggle, from the moment of Grover's death to the awful dying of Ben, makes us aware that isolation and death amount to the same thing for him.

Ironically, his family attachments, which he keenly feels, prevent him from a solitude that might help him realize his creative power. Wolfe could say he cherished as well as feared death because from facing the inevitable he could gain strength. Death must be faced and feared, said Wolfe, claiming those who said they did not fear it were ". . . liars, and fools, and hypocrites." (TWLM, 79) In this early fictional version of his youth, Wolfe presents Eugene as deeply involved with a paradox. Separation is to be feared but also to be cherished. Facing death matures Eugene in a very special way. Each death he endures makes him more capable of coping with his next experience with it. But each event also redeems him; it allows him to begin to understand that death can be seen as something more than a personal experience with the end of a physical process. Gradually from seeing the deaths of loved ones he constructs an analogy that permits him to discern his own life's struggle as a peculiarly personal attempt to conquer death, and at the same time to work his ". . . way toward an essential isolation; a creative solitude; a secret life . . . toward freedom; in a way toward bondage . . . one is as beautiful as the other." (LTW, 111) By the time of Ben's death he can look on dying as a redemptive, not a destructive process.

---

[1] See W. P. Albrecht, "The Titles of *Look Homeward, Angel: A Story of the Buried Life," Modern Language Quarterly,* XI (1950), 50-57. [See pages 97-106 of this collection.]

For subsequent references in the text to the titles of Wolfe's writings, the following abbreviations will be used:

LHA: *Look Homeward, Angel* (New York: Charles Scribner's Sons, 1929).

OTAR: *Of Time and the River* (New York: Charles Scribner's Sons, 1935).

TWR: *The Web and the Rock* (New York: Harper and Brothers, 1939).

YCGHA: *You Can't Go Home Again* (New York: Harper and Brothers, 1940).

TWLM: *Thomas Wolfe's Letters to His Mother, Julia Elizabeth Wolfe,* ed. John Skally Terry (New York: Charles Scribner's Sons, 1951).

LTW: *The Letters of Thomas Wolfe,* ed. Elizabeth Nowell (New York: Charles Scribner's Sons, 1956).

"Eugene thought of death now, with love, with joy. Death was like a lovely and tender woman, Ben's friend and lover, who had come to free him, to heal him, to save him from the torture of life." (LHA, 560)

But this cherishing of death occurs in Eugene only at the end of *Look Homeward, Angel,* and he arrives at this view slowly. Like his father, Eugene fears physical pain and annihilation. Young Eugene's feelings at Grover's death reflect Oliver Gant's earlier response to the death of his first wife, Cynthia, and closely resemble the father's behavior in the presence of other deaths.

Wolfe shows the childish self-pity of Oliver's reactions to all his personal problems, but the father's immaturity appears most obvious in his reactions to the deaths of his first wife and of his sons Grover and Ben. The imminence of Ben's death stimulates him to depths of mawkish self-pity. In tones of ludicrous pathos he wails that Ben's death has come to torture not Ben, but him. Only shortly before his own death can the father face up to his end, as Wolfe shows in *Of Time and the River:* ". . . he knew that he was done for and he no longer cared." (OTAR, 256) But Gant's acceptance of death is an act of precipitate desperation, coming only when he senses ever-nearing Necessity hovering like the Furies about his bed. (258-268)

Not so with Eugene. Since Ben's death he has tried to combat his fear of death by disciplining himself to face it. The degree of maturity he has reached becomes apparent when he decides to break away from home. In his letters Wolfe significantly describes this experience:

> It is like death. I know that people do not die once, but many times, and that life of which they were once a part, and which they thought they could never lose, dies too, becomes a ghost, is lost forever . . . If, then, I am dead to people who once knew me and cared for me, there is nothing more to say or do—I must go on into a new world and a new life . . . (LTW, 216-217)

Unlike his father, Eugene matures with experience, each incident building toward his final achievement. Gant's psychic stagnation contrasts with Eugene's growth. Eugene learns to realize how callous and introverted his father's feelings are. The infantile quality of the father's grief over his first wife parallels the shock and grief of the four-year-old Eugene's response to Grover's death. Neither can get beyond the fear and pain of physical loss. And just as the father is saved from an earlier madness by Eliza, who becomes his second wife, so, ironically, the father, though still suffering himself, can save his son from the darkness weighting down his young mind by the cheerful warmth of the family fire and hearty food. (LHA, 61)

Later when Ben dies, Oliver still shows a pathetic self-centeredness contrasting with Eugene's efforts to gain control of himself. In spite of his fear, Eugene can accept Ben's dying. Alone among the assembly Eugene does not boil over with hate toward others responsible for Ben's death. Only he can quiet his mother whose grief is heightened by Ben's refusal to have her near him. Following their father's example, the others are too concerned with themselves. Although Eugene's "soul plunged downward, drowning in that pit" (548) at his first horror of knowing Ben will die, he controls himself to maintain a selfless awareness of those around him, and from this perception he gains strength. He can finally think of death as a tender, lovely power to be cherished. After this solution Eugene knows the saving grace of humor: he draws the family out of their morbidity soon after Ben's death by reminding them that at least Ben "won't have to drink mama's coffee any more." (559) And he can joke at the artistry of the undertaker who reddens Ben's cheeks with a rouge stick. Wolfe concludes about Eugene in *Look Homeward, Angel*:

> Thus, through the death of his brother, and the sickness that was rooted in his own flesh, Eugene came to know a deeper and darker wisdom than he had ever known before. (587)

This release from his youthful fear of death causes Eugene to think of himself as something unique. He believes that the conquering of his great grief at its very height has made him a new person—a genius, he thinks. From reciting the names of literary greats, military leaders, political emancipators, religious martyrs, he tries to classify himself. The fear of physical death can no longer hold him immobile. After his desperate fantasies conceived to escape from self, he faces the future: "Over that final hedge, he thought, not death, as I once believed—but new life—and new lands." (593)

At this point Eugene benefits further from his father's example. His father had lived a kind of death-in-life since he was unable to escape from the family trap. Eugene must escape this kind of spiritual death that continues to threaten him, for he feels that this death-in-life builds a wall separating him from the new lands. He will not allow himself to sink into the buried life. He must step out of the psychic grave his family lives in. (599-626)

This new life he finds when his mother agrees to send him to Harvard. He dies to one life hoping to be born again. But this escape paradoxically resembles another death, for it leads to another isolation. Yet he now feels willing to face his destiny alone. If this struggle to survive proves fruitless, he will, if necessary, endure spiritual death.

At the end of the novel Ben's ghost advises Eugene to make the voyage to a new life. From facing isolation he may learn that it will bring life to him. Grasping this hopeful vision, Eugene answers:

> I have lost the blood that fed me; I have died the hundred deaths that lead to life. By the slow thunder of drums, the flare of dying cities, I have come to the dark place. . . . And now prepare, my soul, for the beginning hunt. I will plumb seas stranger than those haunted by the Albatross. (625)

The buried life is over, and the angel can look homeward.

In addition to the direct narrative the gradual maturing of Eugene is revealed by two stylistic devices culminating at the death of Ben, the point of Eugene's greatest maturity.

The first device is the persistent references to various kinds of death in preparation for a death scene. It is used in a pattern of association often enough to seem typical of Wolfe's earlier response to the experience. Prior to a death scene, such associations appear abundantly. Then there is a lull in which these references sharply decline. After this lull the scene of dying is narrated. This stylistic pattern occurs for all the death scenes in *Look Homeward, Angel* except the final one, the death of Ben. This break in method suggests the shift in Eugene's point of view.

Three instances of Wolfe's strict adherence to his pattern should suffice: Grover's death, the death of the young prostitute Lily, and the revelation that Oliver Gant is dying of cancer. The prototype is the preparation for Grover's death. From incessant references to death, the subject becomes a leitmotif in the poetic themes of the novel. It is mentioned twenty-three times in the first thirty-five pages, including four euphemisms for death like "the gaunt spectre." (4-35 *passim*) Then occurs the lull of twenty-two pages. The associations with death are allowed to seethe in Oliver Gant's mind. He howls when he learns Eliza plans to leave him since it reminds him of his isolation after his first wife's death. He fears another isolation. Then Grover's death occurs. Although the word "death" is used twice during the four pages narrating Grover's death, it always occurs outside of Eugene's thoughts.

The same pattern leads up to the description of the prostitute's death. (LHA, 265-269) Since the pattern of Grover's death is developed in a span of fifty-seven pages, the same number is considered in examining this second pattern. In this group of pages, the first thirty-five refer to death fourteen times. The next twenty-two pages have only one mention of death. Again the lull is conspicuous. It is also significant that during this lull the horror of isolation is once more emphasized by Gant's knowing that his children are growing up and leaving him. Immediately following this lull, Gant is told of the death of Lily Reed, a young prostitute he knows. Dreading his own impotence and his sure death, Gant sells his cherished Carrara angel to be used for marking her grave.

The familiar pattern appears prior to the pronouncement that Gant is dying of cancer: references to death are often repeated (316-358 *passim*) followed by the characteristic lull that prepares for the revelation of death. The pattern here is only slightly modified, the lull with a single mention of death being only twelve pages long. (358-370) The climax arrives when the surgeon tells his assistant to close the wound because Gant is dying of cancer. No details of a death scene are given. The impact of the doctor's announcement is sufficient. Eugene has sensed his father was dying. Further allusions to it would be artistically and psychologically superfluous.

A secondary device that reveals Wolfe's involvement with the theme of death is his use of poetic allusions to the extent that they become refrains. This method of allusion appears later in the novel than the "death" pattern and is used after it. Primarily it serves only to underscore Eugene's experiences with death, which the first pattern has shown.

In the early chapters the references to literary works mainly record the desultory reading habits of Eugene or his father: popular songs and hymns, Stoddard's lectures, *The Iliad* and *The Odyssey*. After Eugene's fourteenth year, however, the allusions are no longer only records of reading habits and tastes. They begin to appear in a stream-of-consciousness style as Eugene's thoughts and speech suggest the death theme or the life-in-death motif dominating his growth toward maturity. (324-411 *passim*)

This device appears most effectively in Chapters XXIV through XXVII. Here Eugene's reading begins to work its way into his conversation and into his subconscious thoughts. Eugene has read heavily in the Romantics (Coleridge, Keats, Wordsworth, Burns, Scott), the Elizabethans (Shakespeare, Jonson, Dekker), and the Metaphysical and Cavalier poets (Donne, Herrick, Carew, Suckling). (309-315 *passim*) Constant allusions to these poets and their poems show not only how thoroughly he has absorbed his reading but also

his preoccupation with death. The allusions forebode the death of
Ben Gant, pointing to the climactic scene in the novel with artistic
power. The most recurrent allusions in this section are to Ben Jonson
and to Robert Herrick's "Ode to Ben Jonson." (310-344 *passim*)
The other poets alluded to more than once are Keats ("Ode to a
Nightingale") and Coleridge ("The Rime of the Ancient Mariner").
Both of these references are of course particularly appropriate to
the death, death-in-life themes. Poetic allusions appear singularly
effective when they occur in the chapter immediately following
Ben's death. The references become especially frequent to Keats'
"La Belle Dame Sans Merci" and Shelley's "Ode to the West Wind."
(561, 562) These literary echoes serve to intensify the life-in-death,
death-in-life thoughts occupying Eugene's mind at the time. Phras-
ings from these poems course through his mind as Ben's death
dominates the scene. These echoes from the emotions of Keats and
Shelley richly convey the turbulence and insecurity of the other
Gants. Although they have no literary sophistication, they are
probed by Eugene's stream-of-consciousness refrain. Wolfe suggests
through Eugene the aura hovering over the Gants, the aura of death
that will direct their future.

The two devices of using the pattern involving references to death
and repeating poetic passages concerning death generally serve to
suggest the vestiges of immaturity and the approaching maturity in
Eugene's thinking. Overlapping the poetic allusions is the "death"
pattern. But the older Eugene becomes, the less occupied he appears
to be with the fear of an approaching death. Following the doctor's
announcement of Oliver Gant's fatal illness, there is a conspicuous
absence of any reference to death. In effect this section of one hundred and five pages is another lull. Following it, the language of the
novel becomes filled with "death." The story returns to Gant's pain
and his ominous death. Also Ben's existence becomes a virulent sick-
ness; his dark angel hovers above him ceaselessly.

In the meantime, Eugene has gained some maturity. He has gone
off to school, has loved both physically and spiritually, carefully and
carelessly, has become acutely aware of the lost years, the lost faces.
"And there was sorrow in his heart for what would come no more."
(474) This maturing process, giving Eugene some of the perspective
suggested by the evidence of his intellectual sophistication in his
literary responses, occurs during this one-hundred-five-page lull preceding the depiction of Gant's pain, itself a prelude to Ben's death.
Only after these experiences is Eugene more able to face life's problems. The psychological involvement with death becomes less evi-

dent, and the "death" pattern is not used significantly when Bob
Sterling, Eugene's roommate, dies. Eugene is affected by Sterling's
death but he does not ponder it. It is almost irrelevant artistically
except as a signal of Ben's death.

Although Eugene's feelings about death appear repeatedly
through the pages preparing for Ben's death, which Eugene is not
sure he can face, Wolfe has revealed Eugene's increasing strength of
character. For in the summer before Ben's death Eugene has had
experiences that helped him mature even more than his loves and
college life have. Alone in Norfolk and Richmond, he has lived
through a self-imposed isolation and survived. He has thoughts of
his own death during this survival and it has toughened him. (LHA,
521-522)

He can face Ben's death not just to fit Wolfe's stylistic scheme of
varying intensities in feeling but to discover for himself the real
strength he has gained. His response to Ben's death is a final test of
character. Wolfe shows the shift in Eugene both narratively and
stylistically. Eugene is no longer the child who mourned the loss
of physical things and shuddered at ". . . the high horror of death and
oblivion, the decomposition of life." (101) He leaves his childhood in
which he had mourned that men left nothing behind them to keep
their memories alive — something physical, imperishable, like a
tombstone. Now he knows that his father's tombstones are perish-
able. He also outgrows the craning of his neck and the spastic jerks
of his foot lifted suddenly in moments of anguish. The spirit is
stirred but not the body. He can look on his early thoughts of death
as stupid fantasies. (331) Wolfe points to this developing maturity
through the episodes of his novel and two overlapping stylistic devices. As Eugene increases in maturity the complex patterns of
emotional outbursts lessen in number and intensity. After the final
death scene Eugene is ready to face life because he has faced death.
He has risen from the life that buried him and only appeared to be
his real home. He must now search for another father, another
brother, another life. This search Wolfe never completed, for it
continues as a recurring theme throughout his novels. Eugene in *Of
Time and the River* and George Webber in *The Web and the Rock*
and *You Can't Go Home Again* discover it is spiritual death that
is to be feared more than physical death. In *Of Time and the River*
Eugene is seen as struggling to realize spiritual, creative life. Buf-
feted about for a long time, he finally begins to understand what
creativity really is. Then instead of being controlled, he controls. As

the record of *Look Homeward, Angel* closes, Wolfe's hero begins this new struggle in utter isolation. He has only the will to survive.

. . .

Through his protagonists Thomas Wolfe reveals his own maturity after progressing through several stages of feeling toward the attainment of a social ideal. Each step in his emotional development resulted from his becoming less temperamental in responding to environment and friendship. By cleaving instinctively to the American scene, he overcame the disillusionment that plagued his relationships with individuals. Wolfe's responses to his experiences show an achievement of maturity that rejects disillusionment and despair. His concept of death places his fiction outside the stream of contemporary naturalistic fiction, which often, as in Hemingway, cannot rise above the idea of death as nothing but an unreasonable wound, the culmination of an irrational existence.[2] Wolfe has faith even in death since his experience has taught him that it offers a release from an outworn phase of life to a new height of spiritual promise.

---

[2] See Frederick J. Hoffman, "No Beginning and No End: Hemingway and Death," *Essays in Criticism,* III (1953), 73-84.

Louis J. Budd

The Grotesques of
Anderson and Wolfe

From several sources it has become evident that Thomas Wolfe found adolescence less painful than his novels suggest. This indicates that his portrait of Asheville was done from a perspective that he acquired later. But some scholars, now led by Floyd C. Watkins, continue to emphasize his use of names and incidents from his boyhood; others see Wolfe as an exotic artist who fed mainly on his own genius. A few, remembering his academic career, search his novels for borrowings from the great literature of the past. Too little thought has been given to the possibility that his adopted angle of vision parallels that of his literary contemporaries. Following Wolfe's hint, there has been adequate comment on his debt to James Joyce as it appears in the search-for-a-father theme and, somewhat sporadically, in a free handling of narration. No other influences have been argued in detail.

Wolfe's very wide reading included much current fiction besides Joyce; he made shrewd comments about Lewis, Dreiser, Fitzgerald,

From *Modern Fiction Studies*, V (Winter 1959-1960), 304-310. Copyright © 1960 by the Purdue Research Foundation. Reprinted by permission of the Purdue Research Foundation and Louis J. Budd.

and Hemingway. Some of the shrewdest as well as the most approving were about Sherwood Anderson to whose icebreaking letter he replied on July 8, 1935: "You are one of the American writers whose work I have admired most and whose work has meant a lot to me. . . . This comes from the heart. . . ." Anderson, who felt a special affinity with Wolfe, treasured this and later tributes.

Personal friendship led to fuller compliments. After Wolfe had visited Anderson at Marion, Virginia, he wrote on September 22, 1937:

> When I told you how I felt about you and your work, I was not laying it on with a trowel. . . . I think you are one of the most important writers of this country, that you plowed another deep furrow in the American earth, revealed to us another beauty that we knew was there but that no one else had spoken. I think of you with Whitman and with Twain. . . .

A few weeks later an irreparable, confused quarrel erupted. In a hotel lobby, Wolfe—according to what he reported to his secretary— " 'told old Sherwood off,' saying that *Winesburg, Ohio* had meant something important to him and his entire generation of writers, but that Anderson had 'failed them.' " Then, following a riposte from Anderson, Wolfe wrote him for the last time. Surprisingly, he still thought that Anderson's was the "best writing that had been done in this country in this century," and he added, "I shall stick to that. . . ." Considering Wolfe's weakness for devouring animosity, this epitaph is impressive.

If his parting letter had been less generous, it would misrepresent his literary past. Henry T. Volkening, describing a time around 1927, recalls that *Winesburg* stood above Wolfe's working table on the small shelf of volumes that he reread because they contained "much of the best that has ever been written." Likewise, James Boyd reports that when Wolfe came to see him in 1936 he said of Anderson: "He is the only man in America who ever taught me anything. Anything I know of writing I have from him. . . . They will be reading him long after those smart boys are forgotten." Obviously, Wolfe felt a crucial admiration for Anderson's best fiction.

This admiration has been overlooked because Anderson's standing started to slip badly in the later twenties as he failed to pass or even repeat the achievement of *Winesburg.* But for most of the decade he held an almost magnetic position. Lately, William Faulkner has reminded us of his high regard for Anderson during those years, and Hemingway critics have rediscovered a similar tie. In an essay pub-

lished in 1954 so unlikely a disciple as James T. Farrell attests that
Anderson, one of the "most sensitive, significant, and influential of
American writers in this century," had perhaps the profoundest
native influence on him. Anderson was indeed a major figure during
the years that Wolfe switched from drama to fiction; just about
every critic who has commented on Wolfe recognizes this fact and
then develops a contrast between the two. However, Wolfe's praises
for the older man justify a search for a deep-running relationship
that, it turns out, shaped *Look Homeward, Angel* in basic ways.

His earliest letter to Anderson declared: "It seemed to me ever
since I first began to read your books when I was a kid of twenty
that you got down below the surface of our lives and got at some
of the terror and mystery and ugliness and beauty in America better
than anyone else." This meant that he had started to read Anderson
not too long after the appearance in 1919 of *Winesburg*, which in
its dedication spoke of the "hunger to see beneath the surface of
lives." Wolfe was to subtitle his first book "A Story of the Buried
Life." It repeats Anderson's search into the psychic center, into the
most breathing reality—which lies in the emotions that control the
now symbolic actions, not in humdrum and workaday routine. When
Wolfe grandly gave credit to Anderson for "anything I know of
writing," he must have referred partly to this intentness on hidden
feeling.

He had also praised Anderson's evocation of "terror and mystery
and ugliness and beauty." Boyd recalled a simpler comment about
Anderson as "our one sophisticate": "He knows life, all of its ugly
and [its] sweet side better than any of us, but he is not soured. He
takes life as it is and loves it. . . ." In other words, Wolfe deeply
sensed Anderson's unique, complex tone. To the confusion of hometown friends, *Look Homeward* like *Winesburg* highlights the sometimes agonized, sometimes exalted upthrusts through drab normal-
ity. In the note attached to his manuscript as it was being peddled
in 1928, Wolfe insisted that his characters were the "richest and
strangest" yet the "greatest people" he had known and that his
"painful and ugly" treatment of "terror and darkness" vibrated with
a "strong joy." Although some personal bitterness lurked behind
the book's making, he was genuinely disappointed that Ashevillians
should resent it as a betrayal. He intended the same warmth that
ran through *Winesburg;* the theme of life's frightening meaninglessness was linked with a tender belief in life's magic that in Anderson
and Wolfe mounted to a crude religiosity.

The "terror" that Wolfe savored in Anderson's fiction rose primarily from the vision they shared of man's loneliness. People in Winesburg and Altamont have lost their ancestral moorings and their sense of belonging. But the inner man at his best resists annihilation and pursues his right to emotional fulfillment. Painfully, he seeks the unifying word and embrace; too often the violent promptings of his need drive him into self-defeating excesses. However, the chance that he can succeed sets Anderson and Wolfe apart from the psychological realists of the twenties who can promise nothing. The terrible doggedness of the quest in itself affirms human creativity.

Nevertheless, most people meet denials that deform them emotionally. Their plight aroused in Anderson a tenderness that Wolfe magnified into agonized sympathy. Both pitied especially the warping that results when men are baffled in their desire to get truly close to other men. Winesburg has its Elizabeth Willard, Dr. Reefy, Louise Hardy, and Wing Biddlebaum. Altamont has their counterparts in profusion, climaxed by W. O. Gant. His strength never feels honest release, his appetites miss an adequate outlet; he never carves his ideal stone angel or finds peaceful love. Feverish, frustrated Helen is truly his daughter. Ben Gant, like Dr. Parcival's brother, has to retreat behind a contempt that hides his love for Eugene. In its searching, bewildered, and deeply agitated characters, *Look Homeward* is a second "Book of the Grotesque."

Anderson's most influential maneuver had been to make the adolescent his touchstone. With *A Portrait of the Artist as a Young Man* (1916) Joyce swelled the rising tide of novels about sensitive youths. Still, it was Anderson's example that Farrell credited for suggesting a "novel about my boyhood, about the neighborhood in which I grew up." By making the adolescent's struggle toward discovery uncover a common tension between cruelty and understanding, Wolfe stood much closer to Anderson than to Joyce. George Willard and Eugene Gant hope to resolve the dilemmas of feeling by becoming writers; but in their hunger for emotional richness and their ambivalent, often frustrated intercourse with their townsmen, they typify the travail of any innocent spirit. Much more than Stephen Dedalus, they also seem likely to find some day the words of insight that redeem their experiences; leaving the hometown does not mean that they renounce the past.

It is true that their difficulties underscore the small town's failings. Yet, although Wolfe at times imitated the satire of bourgeois

pettiness, his portrait of Altamont was done with a despairing
love not found in Sinclair Lewis's wisecracking cartoons of Gopher
Prairie. Eugene considered Lewis our "best journalist"; however, he
decided that *Main Street* was "like Main Street" in its prejudices
and that *Babbitt* was ludicrously far from being "too strong." *Look
Homeward* is much more like Anderson's mournful study of provincial puritanism and materialism. The lecherous matrons who room
at Dixieland and tipsy, wistful Mrs. Pert, who gives herself to Ben,
are related to Anderson's victims of staid morality. Eliza Gant's
penury and compulsive speculating are grotesquely heightened far
beyond Lewis's smart-aleck satire; she emerges not as a caricature
of the middle class but as a warped being. Like Winesburg, Altamont
is seen through a shocked nostalgia that indicts Main Street's hidden tragedies and deformities much more than its clichés.

This indictment never leaped into a rejection of American society,
however destructive the gap between private needs and public
codes. Ernest Hemingway may hide, as we are told, an inverted love
beneath his flight from this country; Anderson professed a more
open loyalty to the tradition of Lincoln and Whitman. Here again
was Wolfe approvingly perceptive. His first letter praised Anderson's
rendering of life "in America"; his valedictory letter repeated his
gratitude for new vistas on "my country" and "American earth."
Eugene Gant told himself in 1924 that "instead of whining that we
have no traditions . . . we should get busy telling some of the stories
about America that have never been told." In its jabs at our
Anglophiles, in its attempts to give a national backdrop to the
Gants' doings, in its panoramic chapters, *Look Homeward* shows
the old desire to epitomize our best qualities. Anderson and Wolfe
kept a faith in the democratic dream that set them apart from the
expatriate of the twenties; in the proletarian thirties their social
analysis would appeal to native liberalism. If this proves mere
agreement rather than the influence of the older man, it still makes
other borrowings more likely.

Along with the finer similarities in attitude, it makes more rea-
sonable the view that Wolfe followed Anderson in some devices
of method. As belated romantics, they valued emotion and idea
over rigid architecture. Written well within the era of the well-
made novel, *Winesburg* avoids ordered symmetry and *Look Homeward* leans toward shapelessness. Both books approach the effect of
sketches held in the loose autobiographical cycle that Anderson, as
much as anyone, established during the twenties as a prose form.
The tenuous plot line of both is even closer: a boy gropes toward

understanding the quivering inward life of his town; softened by new insight but increasingly restless after the death of a loved member of the family, he takes the train to the shining city and to adulthood.

Indeed, Anderson's penultimate sketch, "Sophistication," foreshadows in detail *Look Homeward's* closing scene. To George Willard, who is about to leave Winesburg, comes a "feeling of loneliness and isolation ... in the crowded streets of his town." He goes out to the empty fairgrounds. "It has itched and squirmed with life and now it is night and the life has all gone away. The silence is almost terrifying. ... One shudders at the thought of the meaninglessness of life while at the same instant ... one loves so intensely that tears come into the eyes." More fully, Anderson generalizes about "every boy when he for the first time takes the backward view of life" as he walks the streets, musing on his future and torn between "ambitions and regrets":

> Suddenly something happens; he stops under a tree and waits as for a voice calling his name. Ghosts of old things creep into his consciousness. ... If he be an imaginative boy a door is torn open and for the first time he looks out upon the world, seeing, as though they marched in procession before him, the countless figures of men who before his time have come out of nothingness into the world, lived their lives and again disappeared into nothingness. ... With a little gasp he sees himself as merely a leaf blown by the wind through the streets of his village. He knows that in spite of all the stout talk of his fellows, he must live and die in uncertainty, a thing blown by the winds. ... The eighteen years he has lived seem but a moment. ... Already he hears death calling. With all his heart he wants to come close to some other human, touch someone with his hands, be touched by the hand of another.

All this in many obvious ways anticipates Eugene's midnight vision in the deserted square of Altamont. Even the style, typical of Anderson's fitful bursts into poetic prose, suggests Wolfe's sonorous, elegaic cadences. Lyric patches are not uncommon in modern fiction, but there is a unique resemblance here that includes symbolism. To those who have wondered about the provenance of the famed cry, "A stone, a leaf, a door," Anderson may supply a partial answer. While the windblown leaf is not used insistently, throughout *Winesburg* the door is his favorite metaphor for the escape from pent-up loneliness.

The temptation to link other books by Anderson and Wolfe is strong. *Windy McPherson's Son* (1916) and *Marching Men* (1917)

deal partly with an adolescent's struggles, sexual stirrings, and grotesque friends, as well as with mute, exalted processions that bear
on Eugene's mystic glimpse of a world "filled with silent marching
men." *Tar* (1926) records an infant's first sensations with a solem-
nity and occasional lyricism that bring to mind the Gants' precocious
son. *Tar*, which Farrell particularly responded to, goes on with the
child's confused feelings toward his parents, his experiences as a
newspaper carrier, and his Eugene-like glimpses of ugliness; it ends
with the boy "racing away out of his childhood" after his mother's
death. From the potpourri of Wolfe's *From Death to Morning* one
may further call "The Far and the Near" a tale after Anderson and
see "In the Park" as imitating his device of naive self-confession.
But any wider argument must remember that in *Of Time and the
River* Eugene's notebook limited a compliment to Anderson with:
". . . he's got too fancy since he wrote *Winesburg, Ohio*."

The tie between Anderson and Wolfe rests mainly on the fact
that while he was still unfledged in writing fiction the younger man
read *Winesburg* with delighted receptivity. He admired its descent
into the hidden emotional world, its counterpoint of terror and
beauty, its poignant sense of man's isolation and the psychic deformities caused by his drive to communicate, its symbolic use of the
adolescent's struggle toward identity, and its somber yet loving
concern with American life. Although Wolfe later complained about
having "every name in the library hurled at my head" and although
he slowly grew away from Anderson, *Winesburg* contributed to the
viewpoint, structure, and even the rhetoric of *Look Homeward*.

Pointing out this influence is worthwhile only so far as it improves
our reading of Wolfe's luxuriant masterpiece, which incontestably
contains teeming proof of his own genius as well as of other borrowings. Awareness of the debt to Anderson better illuminates W. O.
Gant, who could have lived in Winesburg as he "strode muttering
through the streets with rapid gestures of his enormous talking
hands." It better illuminates the "fear and speechless pity" that
Eliza felt when she saw her husband's "small uneasy eyes grow still
and darken with the foiled and groping hunger of old frustration."
It underscores the point that a climactic utterance of *Look Homeward* is her final lament, "We must try to love one another." More
broadly it justifies Wolfe's final tribute to Anderson for seeing
"America with a poet's vision, and with a poetic vision of life —
which to my mind is the only way actually it can be seen." After the
fairly happy years in Asheville and Chapel Hill, Wolfe had looked
back on them with an acquired angle of vision that never aimed at

literal realism. From the vantage point of *Winesburg* we perceive more sharply what he meant us to perceive.

Wolfe's first novel was not a stray meteor. It pages could be aptly illustrated by the earlier watercolors of Charles Burchfield, who profesed a deep artistic obligation to *Winesburg*. For a while the pull toward Anderson's orbit was strong. He attracted those who likewise used the febrile innocent to project a panorama of a society tragically haunted through disregard for emotional needs and who likewise felt, along with the naturalistic desire to cut through taboos, pity and love for redeeming the raw brutalities they uncovered. To include *Look Homeward* in such a grouping helps to explain William Faulkner's high opinion of Wolfe, an opinion that baffles most critics. As we lose our wonder over the uniqueness of *Look Homeward, Angel,* we gain a firmer reading of its meaning for American literature.[1]

---

[1] I wish to thank Professor Walter B. Rideout of Northwestern University for a very intelligent and close reading of an earlier draft of this essay.

John S. Hill

Eugene Gant and the Ghost of Ben

It is readily agreed that Chapter 40 of Thomas Wolfe's *Look Homeward, Angel* is both the goal of the novel and the summation of its author's philosophy. Less agreed upon is the interpretation of this final chapter. The disagreement rises from a faulty explanation of the roles of Eugene and Ben Gant, which, in turn, rests on the misinterpretation of the title. The premise underlying the two erroneous views is, simply: that because Wolfe took this title from Milton's "Lycidas" he also took the explanation. In reality, although Milton can claim the title, it is Wordsworth and Coleridge who claim the content and who influence the final meaning.

The importance of "Lycidas" is further reduced by the history of the novel's title. When Wolfe began writing it in July, 1926, he considered calling the novel *The Building of a Wall.*[1] In November, 1926, he made a list of " 'Possible titles': *The Building of a Wall;*

From *Modern Fiction Studies,* XI (Autumn 1965), 245-249. Copyright © 1965 by the Purdue Research Foundation. Reprinted by permission of the Purdue Research Foundation and John S. Hill.
[1] The facts about Wolfe's titles, as well as the direct quotation concerning them, are found in Elizabeth Nowell, *Thomas Wolfe: a Biography* (Garden City, 1960), p. 111.

Young Poseidon, Poseidon's Harbor, or *Theseus* . . . and *The Hills Beyond Pentland.* . . . By June, 1927, he was considering *Alone, Alone.* . . ." By September, 1927, he settled upon *O, Lost!* It was under this title that the novel was accepted on January 7, 1929, by Scribner's. It was several months later, in the spring of 1929, that Wolfe renamed the novel *Look Homeward, Angel.*

Generally it is valid to assume that because a novelist uses a quotation for his title it is possible to interpret much of the novel in light of the source for the title, as is the case with John Steinbeck's *The Grapes of Wrath* or Ernest Hemingway's *For Whom the Bell Tolls,* to cite only two examples. But with *Look Homeward, Angel* the case is different. And it is precisely this difference which has caused misreading of the final, climactic chapter.

While a graduate student at Harvard, Wolfe studied "The Poets of the Romantic Period" under John Livingston Lowes;[2] Lowes later "praised his thesis on 'The Supernatural in the Poetry and Philosophy of Coleridge.' "[3] Among what Wolfe called "much of the best that has ever been written," he placed "Coleridge (including the essays)."[4] Further, "*The Ancient Mariner* was to become his favorite poem."[5]

Wolfe's motto for the novel, "a stone, a leaf, a door," leads one to Wordsworth's line, "Which, from a tree, a stone, a withered leaf," in *The Prelude* (III, 163). Moreover, the theme of the novel calls to mind Wordsworth's "Ode: Intimations of Immortality from Recollections of Early Childhood" (especially lines 64-65: "But trailing clouds of glory do we come / From God, who is our home") and "My Heart Leaps Up When I Behold" (particularly line seven: "The Child is father of the Man"). Further, "Wolfe's fiction constitutes a search for lost time . . ."[6] and in this respect "Wolfe is close to Wordsworth."[7]

---

[2] Richard S. Kennedy, "Tom Wolfe at Harvard, 1920-1923," *Harvard Library Bulletin* (Spring-Autumn, 1950). This article appears under the title "Wolfe's Harvard Years" in Richard Walser, ed., *The Enigma of Thomas Wolfe: Biographical and Critical Selections* (Cambridge, 1953). Quotation, p. 19. Because Walser's volume includes the revised texts of so many fine articles on Wolfe, subsequent references will, wherever possible, be to Walser as well as to the periodical in which the article first appeared.
[3] Nowell, p. 63.
[4] Henry T. Volkening, "Penance No More," *Virginia Quarterly Review* (Spring, 1939), in Walser, p. 35.
[5] Monroe M. Stearns, "The Metaphysics of Thomas Wolfe," *College English* (January, 1945), in Walser, p. 200.
[6] Louis D. Rubin, Jr., *Thomas Wolfe: The Weather of his Youth* (Baton Rouge, 1955), p. 33.
[7] Rubin, p. 63.

It seems rather obvious that the influence of Wordsworth and Coleridge takes precedence over that of Milton, but this fact is usually mislaid and the final chapter is all too often explained in the light of "Lycidas."

In Chapter 40 of *Look Homeward, Angel*, Eugene Gant encounters the ghost of Ben, his recently deceased older brother, at 3:15 a.m. on the porch of their father's stonecutter's shop, which faces the town square. Throughout the novel, Ben and Eugene are much alike: each represents the individual frustrated in his desire to join his personality to those of all others about him, in his desire to recapture the once better time (so Wolfe believed) from which each one comes, and in his desire to break down the door that prevents man from joining the human race (defined as a single communicating unit) and learning about his own place in the sun.

If one reads this final chapter with "Lycidas" in mind, he will equate Wolfe's refrain, "O Lost, and by the wind grieved, ghost, come back again," with Ben only. From this point it is but a step to an interpretation such as this:

> By analogy Ben's role in *Look Homeward, Angel* would seem to be the angel's, while Eugene is Lycidas; but throughout the novel Ben is also a ghost in that, like every person, he cannot be known even to his brother. In the last chapter he is restored to a "life" he did not have while alive; he is no longer a ghost because no longer a stranger. At the same time he is also an angel in the sense that he can now direct Eugene home. *"You* are your world," says Ben to Eugene, directing him to the bright world of fused experience. Ben is not explicitly named "angel," but the identification is further implied by the stone angels' coming to life when Ben returns.[8]

As one of Wolfe's editors has stated, "he wrote with singleness of purpose, trying to catch in words and fix upon the printed page

[8] W. P. Albrecht, "Time as Unity in Thomas Wolfe," *New Mexico Quarterly Review* (Autumn, 1949), in Walser, p. 243.

Professor Albrecht is close to the truth—but not close enough—in limiting the role of ghost to Ben. Had he said, "Eugene too," he would have been on the threshold of a fine interpretation. He again skirts this point when he says "The title, therefore, is appropriately addressed to Eugene *as well as Ben"* (p. 243; my italics); he is even closer when he sees that "with Ben's return the angels come alive and with them Eugene's creative power" (p. 243), although he has left out any of the reasons for this conclusion.

Professor Albrecht's article is excellent in all other respects, especially in its treatment of the time principle. Perhaps the author was too concerned with another topic ("Time as Unity") to perceive that reliance on "Lycidas" leads one astray in interpreting the all-important final chapter in Wolfe's first novel. If so, he has lots of company.

something deep and dark . . . in human nature."[9] This "something deep" is man's memory (which grows ever dimmer as he ages) of the better land from which he comes; the "something dark" is the steadily growing realization that he cannot return to that land, that home. As such, the now lost land of pre-existence becomes rather like a ghost, and it is for this "lost, and by the wind grieved, ghost" that Eugene yearns. Thus, as will be shown, Eugene and the ghost are synonymous.

Such a reading as this eliminates Ben as *the* ghost; however, he may (for lack of a better term) be called *a* ghost, for such is the accepted term for an apparition. As a ghost, he is like the ghost of Hamlet's father: he imparts information; he does not become the principal character.

There is more than this to Ben's role, however. Throughout the novel, Ben is as alone as Eugene. When he dies, he is still alone. When he returns, it is not merely as an informative ghost but as a part of Eugene himself, as a symbol of what Eugene has discovered through Ben's death.[10]

The apparition of Ben itself limits its role. When Eugene asks "which of us is the ghost"[11] the apparition does not answer. But only a moment later it says, "Fool . . . I tell you I am not a ghost" (p. 517). It is the apparition which asks "What do you want to remember?" and forces Eugene to acknowledge that " 'There is something I have lost and have forgotten.' . . . A Stone, a leaf, an unfound door" (p. 518). In an episode "unwoven from lost time," Eugene sees that

> Ben, in a thousand moments, walked the Square: Ben of the lost years, the forgotten days, the unremembered hours; . . .
> And as Eugene watched . . . he saw himself—his son, his boy, his lost

---

[9] Edward C. Aswell, "An Introduction to Thomas Wolfe," *The Adventures of Young Gant* (New York, 1948). This essay, which appears in this Signet edition (the text is Part II of *Look Homeward, Angel*), was reprinted in the *Saturday Review of Literature* for November 27, 1948. In Walser, p. 107.

[10] The use of a ghost to dramatize the existence of certain knowledge—and its acceptance by a principal character—is not, of course, original with Wolfe. Henry James, for instance, uses this device very well in "The Jolly Corner" when Spencer Brydon encounters a ghost which imparts to him the knowledge of what he really has been like. If one compares them, he will see that although the apparition of Ben is a variation on James's presentation, the central theme is consistent: each author uses an apparition as a symbol of knowledge gained, or to be gained, by the central character.

[11] Thomas Wolfe, *Look Homeward, Angel* (New York, 1952), p. 516. All references to the novel are to this Scribner Library edition and will be cited in the text immediately following the quotations.

and virgin flesh—come over past the fountain . . . And as he passed
the porch where he sat watching, he saw the lost child-face . . .
Eugene leaped to the railing.
"You! You! My Son! My child! Come back! Come back!" (pp.
518-519)

The child is father of the man, yes, but the memory of the child
steadily grows fainter until memory is gone. "Home" to Eugene
Gant is both the land of pre-existence and his own childhood — that
is, childhood as a symbol of hope, of dreams. Heretofore he has
always looked to this home. Now, however, his "meeting with knowledge" (the ghost of Ben) gives him a new home to look toward:
himself.

The fact that the influence upon Wolfe was that of Wordsworth
and Coleridge rather than of Milton; the fact that the title was
selected after, not before, the novel was written; the fact that the
apparition of Ben is a dramatic picturing of Eugene's realization
of certain knowledge; and the fact that the ghost of Ben eliminates
itself as a ghost — all these facts show that it is Eugene, not Ben,
who is the subject of the refrain, "O Lost, and by the wind grieved,
ghost, come back again." Eugene *is* the ghost insofar as the ghost is
a projection of himself — that is, of his past. The lost ghost is the
wispy memory of a once better existence, of a far better place now
grown so dim in memory that it may as well be grieved for only by
the wind. Thus the grieved — for past (the ghost) and Eugene
(whose past it is) are synonymous.

Because the refrain applies so thoroughly to Eugene, it may be
assumed that the "Angel" of the title does too. This assumption is
correct. To revert to Wordsworth for a moment: the already quoted
line, "But trailing clouds of glory do we come / From God who is
our home," indicates what Wolfe first means by "home" and "look
homeward." Further, is not an angel "From God"? Is not an angel
one who trails "clouds of glory"? And if Eugene is the one who seeks
this pre-existence, is he not clearly the angel? Additional proof is
that Eugene is the innocent who receives knowledge; he is the primary seeker in the novel; he is the one who looks homeward, both
to the home that is pre-existence and, later, to home that is in himself. Chapter 40 details the acquisition of knowledge by Eugene —
it is not Ben who looks homeward, for Ben is already there. It is
Eugene Gant who is told to "Look homeward, angel" and who discovers where that home lies. After all, it is not Ben who "turns his
eyes upon the distant soaring ranges" (p. 522).

In Chapter 35, just after Ben dies, Wolfe writes that Ben "lived here a stranger, trying to recapture the music of the lost world, trying to recall the great forgotten language, the lost faces, the stone, the leaf, the door" (p. 465). Far more important, Wolfe also states: "We can believe in the nothingness of life, we can believe in the nothingness of death and of life after death — but who can believe in the nothingness of Ben?" (p. 465).

Obviously, not Eugene. Nor does he believe in the nothingness of himself. This fact is revealed in Chapter 40. The apparition tells Eugene, "*You* are your world" (p. 520) and "*this* is life" (p. 521). At this point, Eugene "stood upon the ramparts of his soul, before the lost land of himself" (p. 521); and he realizes that "no leaf hangs for me in the forest; I shall lift no stone upon the hills; I shall find no door in any city. But in the city of myself, upon the continent of my soul, I shall find the forgotten language, the lost world, a door where I may enter, and music strange as any ever sounded" (p. 521). The novel's final paragraph reinforces the fact that Eugene has new hope, that he has found that the home he must look toward is, indeed, himself: "Yet, as he stood for the last time by the angels of his father's porch, it seemed as if the Square already were far and lost; or, I should say, he was like a man who stands upon a hill above the town he has left, yet does not say 'The town is near', but turns his eyes upon the distant soaring ranges" (p. 522).

Throughout the first thirty-nine chapters of *Look Homeward, Angel,* Eugene Gant longs for the home from which he came. In Chapter 40 he discovers that he holds the answers to his questions within himself. He learns this through the apparition of Ben, which is a dramatic projection of his own thoughts and his conclusions about them. Eugene accepts this knowledge, as all men must, and faces the future with confidence. Eugene, who did not believe in the nothingness of Ben, certainly does not, in the final summary, believe in the nothingness of Eugene Gant, either.

Louis D. Rubin, Jr.

From "Thomas Wolfe: Time and the South"

Thomas Wolfe was born in Asheville, North Carolina, in 1900. His origins and upbringing were squarely lower middle class. All the other writers of the modern South came from families that were among the cultural leaders of the community, the Southern squirearchy, with its antebellum roots. Not so Wolfe; his father was a stonemason from Pennsylvania, a man who worked with his hands and was proud of it—though, as his son several times reminds us, he always wore a starched collar and tie on the job, with an apron pulled up over his good clothes to protect them from the dust. His mother's people, the Westalls, were a numerous mountain family; many of its members had come down to the town at about the time of the Civil War. They were "new people," and had no strong ties with the pre-War Southern aristocracy. Some of them grew quite wealthy during the late nineteenth and early twentieth centuries. Thomas Wolfe was the first member of his immediate family to go to college; he wanted to go to the University of Virginia or to Van-

From *The Faraway Country: Writers of the Modern South,* by Louis D. Rubin, Jr. Copyright © 1963 by the University of Washington Press. Reprinted by permission of the University of Washington Press and Louis D. Rubin, Jr.

derbilt—it is interesting to speculate on what might have happened had he been sent to the latter school—but his father insisted that he attend the state university in Chapel Hill.

When we look at Eugene Gant's childhood as pictured in *Look Homeward, Angel,* what is most striking about it is its cultural impoverishment. There were a few books in the house—of poems, the obvious ones, for his father liked to declaim sentimental verse—but of literary and artistic interest there was almost none, save perhaps his sister's ambition to be a successful popular singer. A scene in *Look Homeward, Angel* describes how Eugene Gant, inspired by the tercentenary of the death of William Shakespeare, affixes a portrait of the poet to the wall, scrawling under it Ben Jonson's words, "My Shakespeare, rise!" He is tortured about it thereafter by the family: "Will My Shakespeare pass the biscuits?" and so forth. Despite the humor, however, an element of pathos is apparent in the episode. It shows us something of the kind of understanding a young man of Wolfe's temperament and interests must have received from his family.

Mrs. Wolfe ran a boardinghouse, a sprawling, cheaply constructed affair with bare, calcimined walls and poorly lighted halls. Jonathan Daniels describes how Wolfe's body lay in state in the boardinghouse after his death in 1938. The coffin, he writes,

> filled half the front room, which was hall also, of the old boardinghouse. Above it there were long cracks in the yellow plaster ceiling. He was home.
> "Those melancholy cracks in the yellow plaster looking down at him!" the woman who was his friend said. "I know he fled from those cracks, and there he lay helpless while they triumphed over him."

The observation was an apt one; Wolfe's childhood was a time of much ugliness, and sometimes the depiction of Altamont that we read in *Look Homeward, Angel* is as bleak, as barren, as unlovely as any description in the work of the Midwestern naturalistic novelists such as Dreiser and Anderson. Eugene Gant's career, no less than Thomas Wolfe's, was a search for loveliness, for aesthetic joy. He dreamed of the shining city beyond the mountains, where all would be radiant and beautiful. In 1923 he wrote from Harvard to his mother, about the plays he was going to write:

> What I shall try to get into [people's] dusty, little pint-measure minds is that a full belly, a good automobile, paved streets, and so on, do not make them one whit better or finer,—that there is beauty

in this world,—beauty even in this wilderness of ugliness and provincialism that is at present our country, beauty and spirit which
will make us men instead of cheap Board of Trade Boosters, and
blatant pamphleteers. . . .

The life that Eugene Gant knows as he grows up, from his childhood to the moment when he prepares to leave Altamont for the
golden city, involves drunkenness, violence, drabness, pain, penury,
death. His recoil from the ugliness of so much of his environment
is into himself; by his twelfth year, we are told, he has learned to
"project mechanically, before the world, an acceptable counterfeit
of himself which would protect him from intrusion." He is sent out
early to earn money, first by selling magazines, then by delivering
newspapers in the early morning on the Niggertown route. His
mother is preoccupied with real estate; his father, grown old and
sick, engages in periodic violent drinking bouts from which he stag-
gers home, reeling and cursing.

Sent to a private school, Eugene comes under the protection of
the wife of the principal, who mothers him and reads poetry to him.
It is an oasis of beauty in a wilderness of drabness and pain:
"Against the bleak horror of [the boardinghouse], against the dark
road of pain and death down which the great limbs of Gant had
already begun to slope, against all the loneliness and imprisonment
of his own life which had gnawed him like hunger, these years at
Leonard's bloomed like golden apples." At school he reads Wordsworth, Burns, Shakespeare, Jonson; meanwhile his father is dying,
his brother Ben growing more aloof and bitter each year, his sister
Helen off singing in theaters somewhere.

Yet set against the cultural impoverishment of family life and
the town, the barrenness of the boardinghouse, is the outdoor world,
the mountains that ringed Altamont, nature, the seasons. This
aspect, largely missing in the novels of the Midwestern naturalists,
is abundantly present in Wolfe. Frequent episodes are given over
to the description of natural beauty, the coming and going of the
seasons in the Carolina mountains: "Spring lay abroad through
all the garden of this world. Beyond the hills the land bayed out to
other hills, to golden cities, to rich meadows, to deep forests, to the
sea. Forever and ever." In nature, and through his imagination,
Eugene escaped from "the dim fly-specked lights, the wretched
progress about the house in search of warmth, Eliza untidily wrap-
ped in an old sweater, a dirty muffler, a cast-off man's coat." In the
twenty-fourth chapter of *Look Homeward, Angel*, Eugene walks

downtown. It is a humorous chapter, quite unlike the bleak naturalistic depictions of wretched prairie towns by Dreiser, Anderson, and
Lewis. The portrait is done not in harshness and viciousness, but in
affection and joy for the people and places seen and known. We
must not forget this when we discuss Wolfe's attitude toward the
community in which he grew up: there is attraction and revulsion,
pleasure and pain, and their often contradictory mixture is essential
to an understanding of Wolfe.

Look Homeward, Angel is a chronicle novel, describing the first
twenty years of Eugene Gant's life. It is dominated by the passing
of time. Old Gant is dying; the family is falling apart; Eugene is
growing up. Everywhere is the massive fact of change. The Gants
are always in a state of turmoil. Eliza sets up a separate establish-
ment at the boardinghouse, busies herself with real estate. Early
in the novel Grover dies; much later on Ben too dies. Helen marries
and leaves. Eugene goes off to college. Of stability and certainty
there are almost none. The only fixed element is Eugene's own consciousness, and that too changes and expands as he becomes an
adolescent and discovers sex, desire, art. Even as a child he had
stared at a baby picture of himself, and "turned away sick with
fear and the effort to touch, retain, grasp himself for only a moment."
The novel is a series of episodes strung out in time: almost every
chapter of *Look Homeward, Angel* contains in its first paragraph
a reference to the flight of time and the coming and going of the
seasons.

Occasionally the characters observe themselves caught in time,
and can only look with awe and fear at what they see. Old Gant sells
the stone angel of his youth to adorn a prostitute's grave, then steps
out onto the porch of his monument shop. For an instant all life in
the town square below seems suspended, "and Gant felt himself
alone move deathward in a world of seemings. . . ." At the very close
of the novel, when Ben has died and Eugene has completed college
and is preparing to depart for the North, he stands on the porch
of the shop exactly as Old Gant had done, and converses with the
ghostly shade of Ben. The fountain in the square is suddenly motionless, frozen in time. The stone animals of the monuments get up
and walk. All that he has seen and known parades before Eugene's
unbelieving eyes. Then, in the climactic moment of the novel, he
sees, coming along past the fountain carrying his load of newspapers,
"himself—his son, his body, his lost and virgin flesh." His own childhood self passes by, the self lost in time, vanished down the years.
Eugene calls to him. "His voice strangled in his throat; the boy

had gone, leaving the memory of his bewitched and listening face turned to the hidden world. O lost!" So swiftly has it all happened, almost without his knowing it; he has grown to manhood, and whatever he once was is lost and unrecapturable. Time, chronology, change; these are the only reality he knows. Then the fountain begins splashing again, and the novel is concluded.

There are two narrative progressions in *Look Homeward, Angel.* Eugene, as we have noted, is born within the community, grows up, and prepares to leave. His father comes to the community from the outer world, becomes increasingly trapped within it, struggles vainly to escape, grows old and sick, will soon die there. This dual movement, into and away from Altamont, constitutes the structure of the novel. W. O. Gant is the frustrated mortal, the lonely American never acquiescent in his lot, who wanders from childhood onward, drifting to Altamont by chance, taking up residence there, marrying a woman he does not love deeply, fathering children, growing old and sick, and finally waiting to die. As a boy he had learned stonecutting; he wanted to carve an angel, but his skill was sufficient only for lettering monuments. He keeps a stone angel on the porch of his shop, curses it, reviles it; it is a reminder of what he wanted to do and be. Finally he sells it to adorn the grave of a prostitute. *Look Homeward, Angel* is subtitled "A story of the buried life," and Old Gant's life is buried, hidden under the debris of the years. "Where now? Where after? Where then?" Wolfe asks after Gant sells the statue and watches the town square grow still.

Important though W. O. Gant's journey is, *Look Homeward, Angel* is his son Eugene's book. It is seen through his consciousness. We do not need the foreword "To the Reader" to tell us that the point of view is that of Eugene looking backward. The meaning and unity of all the events in the novel lie in their impact on Eugene, not only the Eugene who grows up in the book, but the Eugene who is remembering it all. Eugene is the youngest son of W. O. and Eliza; as his father grows old, he grows to manhood. His early years are filled with conflict—between his father and mother; between the claims of the Woodson Street home his father owns and the boardinghouse his mother buys and operates; between Altamont's small-town ways and its ambitions to become a metropolis; between the conservative instincts of the society and the boomtown atmosphere of everyday life; between his own artistic leanings and the thoroughly middle-class attitudes toward such interests held by his family and the townsfolk.

As the novel develops, so does Eugene's gradual estrangement from family and community. The death of Ben culminates the process of Eugene's alienation from the family. His developing aesthetic and intellectual interests, his revulsion from trade and business, his growing ambition separate him from his fellow townsmen. Hatred of the ugliness and pettiness of small-town life causes him to withdraw into his own consciousness; after Ben is gone his isolation is almost complete. The Eugene who looks not townward but toward the distant hills at the conclusion of the novel is done with life in Altamont; his gaze is on the shining city, the promise of artistic achievement. He will avoid the entombment within the town that his father suffered, the emotional suffocation that was Ben's lot, for unlike them he will be saved by his genius, by the miracle of his art. (That his best art would be the recreation of life in the same town is an interesting irony, and not unimportant to what the town meant for Wolfe.)

The midway point in the process of alienation, it seems to me, is the part of the twenty-fourth chapter, mentioned previously, that describes Eugene as he leaves Leonard's school with his friend George Graves and walks into the city. Laughing and bantering as he goes, Eugene sees the people, places, and events of Altamont life as in a moment of stasis, before his own vision has become so subjective that it will permit him to see things only as they affect his private identity. It is a matchless portrayal of a small city's downtown area, one neither distorted by adult prejudgments nor overly simplified by a child's naïveté. Afterward Eugene will discover sex, and love, and death, and art, and never again will he be able to look at Altamont with so much objectivity as he does on that day. It is the halfway mark; before it comes, Eugene is a small child, still largely unseeing; afterward he is a preoccupied, self-centered adolescent, caught up in his moods and desires. Just once, in this chapter, Altamont is seen whole. Thereafter Eugene is growing away from it too rapidly to look at it for what it is.

. . .

In the later fiction the narrowness of Wolfe's viewpoint, the subjectivity with which he viewed his experience, was a crippling disability, for he could not describe a man living among other men in a convincing fashion. There are only fragments, moments of illumination. But *Look Homeward, Angel* is bathed in color and light from beginning to end. The child's world he saw whole, and although Eugene Gant is in conflict with it almost from the outset, this did not prevent Wolfe from describing that world with great fervor and vividness. The fabric of a small city's life is unrolled before us. We see its workings, its hold on its inhabitants, especially on the Gants who live there. We see a Southern community in the toils of transition, growing from a small mountain town into a busy tourist city; we see the inhabitants adjusting to accommodate themselves to the change. The members of the Gant family embody the process. Eliza Gant, the canny, conservative, slow-moving mountain woman, becomes the real-estate speculator, the woman of property, who participates zestfully in the commercial mania. Luke Gant takes to the business world with great success. Ben Gant yearns for a home, love, certainty, and dies without them. W. O. Gant, a violent, tumultuous person, comes from the outside, settles down, but finds no peace for his mind. Eugene, born into the community as it is changing, is caught up in the process, cannot find a place for himself, and leaves to pursue his art in the shining city.

It is the process of the change that is foremost, and means most to Eugene and to Wolfe. From childhood Eugene is conscious of time and change. Finally these become the only reality, the only logic and order he can find for what he has known and been. Thus Wolfe wrote his novel of change and alienation. A boy grows up in a Southern town and goes off into modern America, leaving behind him death, taking with him only the memory of the past. So terribly and so indelibly had the process of alienation marked him that the art he went away to pursue became one of recapture, of searching the memories of the past for whatever reality there might be in life.

He was a thoroughgoing Romantic; his writing has the intensity of fiction written by an artist who is seeking furiously, through his literary craft, to impose on his recalcitrant experience his own highly personal valuations. This is the way it was! he insists, and in order to convince us of the justice of his contention, he marshals the force and excitement of a tremendous rhetorical talent. It is his chief concern in *Look Homeward, Angel*, his self-appointed mission: to recreate the circumstances of his childhood, to give to his chaotic experience the order and the importance of a work of art. He wrote a beautiful tale of growth and alienation, in which he, who had experienced it and known both, was the chief character. He recaptured the past, recreated his family, his community, himself, the love and the pain he had felt there, and the loss he knew as he saw it vanish in time.

So far as any American fiction endures, Altamont endures, in motionless vision, timeless chronology. In one great novel Thomas Wolfe fixed the transient world he knew so well into changeless art.

Pamela Hansford Johnson

The Incommunicable Prison

"Like a tipsy undergraduate . . . announcing . . . that there is a 'something somewhere if we can only find it' " Wolfe certainly was; but with this difference, that his search for the "something somewhere" continued into sobriety and never ceased. However vain a quest, it was not an ignoble one. Wolfe experienced more often than most people that flash of light just beyond the edge of vision which is accompanied by the conviction that "the whole thing is there," if only one could turn one's head quickly enough to catch it. He knew the sensation of a single supreme idea nearly formulated, then lost forever; an idea which, once crystallised, would be sufficient to change and irradiate the entire thought of the world. The experience is not unlike a sudden, violent and inexplicable thirst. He knew that we are imprisoned in the shell of our flesh, and that we cannot speak the words which would set us free; that mankind is hopelessly inarticulate, able to record in speech only the most broken chart of his thought.

From *Hungry Gulliver: An English Critical Appraisal of Thomas Wolfe*, by Pamela Hansford Johnson, published by Charles Scribner's Sons. Copyright © 1948 by Pamela Hansford Johnson. Reprinted with the permission of Charles Scribner's Sons and Lady Snow.

> Could I make tongue say more than tongue could utter! Could I
> make brain grasp more than brain could think!

All his life Wolfe tried to do this impossible thing, and in trying
burned himself out. His entire work is a forcing process. With every
word he wrote he was trying to say more than any human being
had ever said of the marvel of the earth and of man. He wanted to
capture in words the experience of *nearly understanding* and, more
preposterous and more wonderful, to be the first man in all the
world to understand completely. This was the ideal by which he
lived and by which he laboured, an unsophisticated, incorrupt and
terrifying ideal. A child might have conceived it, as a child might
simply have conceived the desire to be, some day, the greatest man
that ever lived.

> The deepest search in life, it seemed to me, the thing that in one
> way or another was central to all living, was man's search for a
> father, not merely the father of his flesh, not merely the lost father
> of his youth, but the image of a strength and wisdom external to his
> need and superior to his hunger, to which the belief and power of his
> own life could be united.

Yet all Wolfe succeeded in producing was a history of violent
endeavour. At the end he knew his questions were yet unanswered,
and that he had come no nearer to the "something somewhere"
than he had been in the days when he was writing his one-act plays.
Proust, who would never have contemplated an odyssey such as
Wolfe's, came infinitely nearer to achieving Wolfe's desire. The
incidents of the dipped madeleine and of the stumble at the unex-
pected step are both transcriptions of an intense and familiar human
experience: as no man before him he caught it, analysed it, and
related it to the past. Proust, seeking to explain the personal miracles that are rooted in time past, and Wolfe, seeking to explain
the personal miracles which he feels must be leaning down to him
from stems that are rooted in the future, were working to opposite
ends, yet Proust, in his deadly patience, penetrated further into
the incommunicable prison than Wolfe in his gigantic fury.

When Wolfe died his work was done. It is all there, ended as
surely as a work of music is ended by the last downward cut of the
baton. Had he lived, he would have gone on writing; but becoming
always more confused as he faced a second world war that must
have set him in hopeless conflict with himself.

It is no accident that *Look Homeward, Angel* is the most clear-sighted of his novels. Born into the lower middle-class life of a small mountain town, he pictured the familiar world with an objectivity altogether remarkable. The farther he journeyed from Asheville the more baffled he became, and the less sure of himself. When he left the mountains he discovered that he could not go home again, and for the rest of his life was haunted by the sense of being a wanderer and adrift. He was lost in the city and in the foreign lands; in 1929 the whole world of his most intimate experience came to an end, and he never came to terms with the new one. In his loneliness he was America herself, America of the nineteen-twenties: huge, young, aggressive, unfound, like an adolescent at a grownup party, and he looked with desire and awe upon the future. He managed to "greet the unseen with a cheer," proclaiming his certainties, thundering his reassurances; but he was never again as confident of himself as Eugene had been when he spoke with Ben's ghost beneath the stone angel.

With all his gigantic faults, his prolixity, his ranting, his stupefying absurdities, Wolfe is incomparably the most significant figure in three decades of American literature. His egotism arises from a profound desire to analyse the nature of his own being, not from a passion to display himself to others. He is the egotist unconscious of an audience. Hemingway, for all his sophistication, his taste, his superb selectivity, always gives an impression of being aware that company is present and that he is responsible for its entertainment. He is permanently on his mettle, eyes and ears sharpened, alert for the least sign of weariness or irritation. Wolfe is labouring upon a mental excavation that engages his entire attention; he would no sooner make a concession to an interruptor than a surgeon would break off in the middle of trepanning to look out of the window at a Salvation Army band.

He never acquired "poise." His later work displays even more sharply than his earlier books the defiance that comes of being uncertain. His antagonism towards modern European culture sprang from worshipful envy of its long ancestry. By his references to "fancy" writing, he means the oversophisticated writing of the intellectual who believes fundamentally that his learning has made him superior to the common man; and this is a peculiarly European outlook. Wolfe felt that the foundations of an American literature were still being laid; and he therefore resented the writer whose ease arises out of a conviction that he is simply continuing, and adorning, a tradition. The youthfulness of his country weighed heavily upon Wolfe; he thought of America *culturally* as the brilliant but underprivileged board school boy matched against the university man of Europe—a boy who, because of his very disadvantages, must work twice as hard and succeed three times as brilliantly.

He never acquired "professionalism." He never learned to trim his work, polish it, or play safe with it. He was never able to make himself comfortable at literary parties. He wrote because he wished to communicate something that seemed to him inexpressibly urgent; nothing else mattered. This is why his books carry so powerful a sense of his personality; they are the most intimate writings, the most naked and the most trustful, of this generation. He set out in search of an impossible ideal—to communicate that which is incommunicable. He ended with a philosophy that is little more than a few vague conclusions and a few verifications. What he did achieve was a finished portrait of the artist as a young man, and within this man the portrait of a continent. "The whole thing's there—it really *is*."

The artist is a small-town boy of remarkable physical and mental attributes, and the ambition of a Caesar. The niggling life of home drives him into a frenzy of revolt; he thrashes about like a whale, striking wildly at everyone and everything, yet holding in reserve that one last element of bitterness which might make retreat impossible. Struggle as he may against the family unit, he is forever bound to it. His head is giddy with the riches of a vast reading, and his daydreams are created out of literature rather than by any observation of romantic love at close quarters—in fact, he has seen none, and the marriages of Altamont freeze him to the bone. When ambition takes him to the city, he is inhibited by the consciousness of his own provincialism. He is Ulysses without a ha'porth of faith in Penelope, contemptuous of her and of her smart friends. The world outside America defeats him because he believes in the power of kinship above all things, and is most tied by it; and when a people to whom he considers himself kin passes into a state of corruption, he is thrown into bewilderment and despair. Politically (so far as he is political at all) he might have veered towards a romantic fascism, if it were not that he is basically objective and absolutely *kind*.

Socially he is unreliable, the guest whose problematical behaviour fills the prospective hostess with apprehension. A fancied slight will move him to sullenness or to insult. Though he gets drunk in the grand manner, he is really a poor drinker, and a small amount of alcohol will unbalance him. Among women he searches for a mother; and when he finds one, and has been mothered to satiety, he breaks free of her loving with signal violence. He likes to believe himself harsh and self-reliant. In fact, he cares deeply about what people say of him. He resents the whimsical, the sly, the "delicate" as a boy resents some "girlish" gift or occupation.

(Oddly enough, Wolfe greatly admired Sir J. M. Barrie.

I think Barrie is the most significant dramatist in the English-speaking world to-day because he really is carrying on the great tradition of our dream. This is an arch-heresy here where some of my young critical friends consider him "sentimental." Is it not strange how the academic, critical point of view shrinks nervously away from the sympathetic? I have never read a play of Barrie's that didn't give me this curious "mixed" feeling. He is not trying to "prove" anything (thank Heaven) but like Shakespeare and other old fogies, is more interested in the stories of human beings than in the labor problem. That's why I believe his plays will outlast those of his contemporaries, because people at all times can understand and appreciate the emotion of other people.[1]

This feeling for Barrie consorts queerly with Wolfe's outbreaks against the "elfin" touch; it is possible that his admiration for Barrie's fine technical qualities blurred his perception of the philosophy behind the plays. Logically, Peter Pannishness should have infuriated him because, though Wolfe longed to break out of boyhood into full maturity, he could never quite achieve the transition; while Peter Pan actually wishes to remain in the irresponsible and subordinate state of being a child.)

The artist is oppressed by the limitations, not only of his own powers of verbal expression, but of any man's. He longs for the gift of tongues, that he may make all things clear to the whole of the world. He believes in the existence of absolute goodness and absolute evil—in everything, in fact, that is large and plain and incontrovertible. He believes that the best thing to do in face of darkness and doubt is to state a creed at the top of the voice, and then trust to luck. The cicada America, sloughing off her dead shell, would emerge beautiful and new into the dazzling air of morning.

I believe that we are lost here in America, but I believe we shall be found.

---

[1] "Letter to Mrs. Roberts," *The Atlantic Monthly* (December, 1946).

Man was born to live, to suffer and to die, and what befalls him is a tragic lot. There is no denying this in the final end. *But we must, dear Fox, deny it all along the way.*

Believe: that is the only word the prisoner has discovered after his life sentence in the cell of flesh. Had he for one moment entertained the slightest hope of success it would be a confession of failure, but he knew, before he died, that the search had been an end in itself.

The most striking feature of the Gant-Webber novels is their youthfulness. They do, indeed, look outward upon the future as a boy looks out in fear and terrifying hope upon his manhood. Their sincerity is a boy's sincerity, and their confidence is that friendliness which is offered to all men only before experience has brought common sense and distrust, balance and corruption.

When *Look Homeward, Angel,* was first published in England, it was the young people who greeted it with excitement and with that curious uprush of personal affection which upon rare occasion greets the author of a novel that has come upon certain hidden springs in the wilderness of the reader's desire. Young men and women between seventeen and twenty-three years of age felt that in some obscure way Wolfe was their spokesman; perhaps, after all, he had managed to send out some message from the incommunicable prison. His lyricism was the expression of their own longing to put into words the wonder and strangeness of coming out of childhood. The Laura James idyll which, to the mature critic, shows Wolfe at his weakest, to the adolescent represented love as he most deeply wished to find it. The boy who felt himself in any way restrained or subjected by his parents was moved by Eugene's protest to his family after the fight with Luke and Ben; this, thought the boy, is what *I* should like to have said, if only I could have found the words. The optimism towards the future, *despite the gainsaying of a dead man,* encouraged the young reader to feel himself Promethean, capable of defying not only those set in authority over him by reason of kinship, age and experience, but of defying also the supernatural authority—God and the voice of the Prophets. Wolfe gave to the young man a conviction that whatever might be the defeat of others, his own future would be straight and shining as the path of the sun across the sea.

In his lifetime Thomas Wolfe made an international reputation. A great deal of critical attention has been devoted to his work in America and in Germany also, but already the colours of his fame are beginning very slightly to dull. In a sense England and America have still to discover him. He has his place with Hemingway, Faulkner and Steinbeck in the histories of American literature; but only as one modern writer among others. His comparative importance is as yet unassessed.

Beside him Faulkner appears neurotic and obscure, Hemingway oversophisticated and Steinbeck, a novelist of power and solidity, to have a certain recessive quality, as if his people and his places were set a little way back from the full lights of the reader's vision. Faulkner's "Southness," so much deeper than Wolfe's, perverts his vision like a black scarf tied over one eye. Though he lacks Wolfe's ear for words and indulges in bouts of word juggling that not infrequently degenerate into nonsense, he is the more mature writer of the two; but he lacks Wolfe's humanity and affectionate understanding of ordinary people. Steinbeck, an expert craftsman who has achieved a mature philosophy and has something vital to say, sees humanity rather than human beings. No Steinbeck character is completely an individual, but typifies a group. Because of this, the force of the message itself is weakened; we always believe something a friend tells us firsthand rather than something we read in the newspapers, and what Tom Joad has to say would have gripped the attention even more straitly if Joad had been a man we could have recognised instantly (not only as a type but as a single human being) had we met him on the street. Wolfe, who is infinitely less ordered a thinker than Steinbeck and with far less of real importance to communicate, never drew a character who was not visible even to the lines in the palm of the hand, whose voice was not audible even to the lowest mutter of speech, whose behaviour in any set of circumstances could not be anticipated with certainty to the last gesture.

Faulkner, Steinbeck and Hemingway, despite their powerful consciousness not merely of adding to but of building a national culture, could easily have been Europeans. They look upon Europe with a sympathy unclouded by the jealousy or sense of "inferiority" that was ineradicable in Wolfe. They are, in fact, grown-up, while he remains rooted in adolescence. In spite of his prejudices, Wolfe brings to Europe a curiously sharp understanding, though this tends to embrace the colours, scents and weathers, the whole "feel" of a country, rather than its people. He views the English nervously, the French with a degree of contempt, and speaks warmly of the Germans alone.

He is American as Whitman was American, and like Whitman realises the *earliness* of the time at which he speaks. Although he cannot claim, as Whitman could, to be among the pioneers, he does believe himself in the company of those who follow after them to develop the ore and oil of a new continent. His tremendous pride, the pride that vented itself in hostility towards the friends of Esther Jack, towards the English, and towards the publishers "Rawng and Wright," is counteracted by an even greater joy in being young, in being uncertain, of sitting down with the primer and learning the world from the beginning as once he learned new languages. Alone among the writers of his generation he understands that the indigenous culture of his country today is as young as England's was when Chaucer struck open the great way of modern English letters, and that the spaces of her future are unbounded.

Thomas Wolfe

Epilogue: In Retrospect

About my book the only apology I have to make is that it is not better—and by "better" I mean that it does not represent by any means the best of which I am capable. But I hope I shall feel this way about my work for many years to come. But there is much in this first book for which I hope I shall always continue to feel affection and pride.

I can not go into explanations of the creative act. That has been done many times by other people, and much better than I could hope to. I can only assure you that my book is a work of fiction, and that no person or no act or event has been deliberately and consciously described. But I think you know that fiction is not spun out of the air, it is made from the solid stuff of human experience. Dr. Johnson said a man would turn over half a library to make a book; so may a novelist turn over half a town to make a figure in his novel. This is not the only method, but this is illustrative, I believe, of the whole process.

From *The Notebooks of Thomas Wolfe,* edited by Richard S. Kennedy and Paschal Reeves. Copyright © 1970 by The University of North Carolina Press. Reprinted by permission of The University of North Carolina Press, and Richard S. Kennedy and Paschal Reeves.